The Kith and Kin of Hanumaan

Shreedharaa

Copyright © 2025
All Rights Reserved

Dedication

This write-up is dedicated to the writer's mother and father, who as exemplary homo-sapiens were polar opposites in all their characteristics, - but who, despite having very little money between them, maintained a 100% commitment to non-violence and truthfulness in all aspects of their lives.

This write-up is also dedicated to all those **who truly understand** that the most dedicated effort required of each one them is to themselves and their *group members*, most notably to their progeny starting from the very moment of their birth; - that each one of them become trained and convinced in the solid understanding that all things in this universe are results of natural processes, and there is absolutely nothing that is supernatural.

(In the mildest form for youngsters, a kid can have a cuddly, soft toy of a horse with a horn, but the kid should be told that there

is no such living creature anywhere in the world. There is no such figure as the tooth fairy, nor is there a jolly, friendly old man with a white beard bringing gifts in the middle of the night each year.)

Even the tiniest brains of ants or bees have figured out how to cooperate as groups for all their living activities using the never-ending process of their evolution to their advantage. There's no excuse for us homo-sapiens to make excuses *for killing each other*. This write-up is also dedicated to all homo-sapiens of any place, any creed, any culture or language who understand that their brains are large enough to figure out living cooperatively while cooperatively taking care of the environment.

About the Writer

The writer grew up in a *heavily foreign-controlled* East Asian colonial country.

A supremely cocky, arrogant, spoiled and obnoxious but "perennial grade-A" student that he was, he did not realize that there were countless other homo-sapiens of his caliber and better, after he moved to a powerful western country for further education. Further education he surely got! Soon enough, he learned that he had to change his ways. Embracing this humbling necessity, perpetual changing became a full-time, lifelong effort for him, and he accepted it.

Terminology and other nuances as used in this write-up with intended meaning:

The writer frequently quotes a line from famous songs of **the Fab-Four** for entertainment only.

5k=5,000 years, 10k=10,000 years, 6m=6 million years *and so on*.

The Evolutionary Modern Era (=10k) refers to the period going back from this year to 10,000 years, i.e. the last 10k years.

Hominin means a biped chimp that has evolved to be something human like, to some indefinite extent.

Homo-sapien(s) is used to refer to "**us**" as we are today, singular or plural.

Homo-penultimate is the hominin species just prior to homo-sapien. – could be Neanderthals.

Homo-*whatever* is hominin species at any particular time in the 6m years of hominin evolution. The final homo-*whatevers* is "us" and the penultimate to us *is probably* homo-neanderthalensis. Homo-*whatevers* is plural form.

Any comment of any type can be addressed with your name and return address included "by snail mail on paper" to:

Shreedharaa, P O Box 39034, Chicago, IL, USA 60639

While "it" is the normal "it", "**IT**" refers to adult male and female doing "**IT**". Get it?

god-etc. is often used, to be interpreted to mean *any and all supernatural beliefs*, profound or childlike, such as: - god, creator, - faith, - afterlife, - heaven, - hell, - reincarnation, - rebirth, - miracles, - prayers, -chants, - sacrifices, -deities, -rituals, zodiac signs etc. (including childlike unicorns, ho-ho-ho homo-sapien with gifts in the middle of night, -tooth fairy, etc.)

He can mean he-or-she, **His** can mean his-or-her, but **she** means only she, **her** means only her

Caretakers generally refers to parents, but can also mean those entrusted with parenting, with legal guardianship and any such.

Page left Blank Intentionally

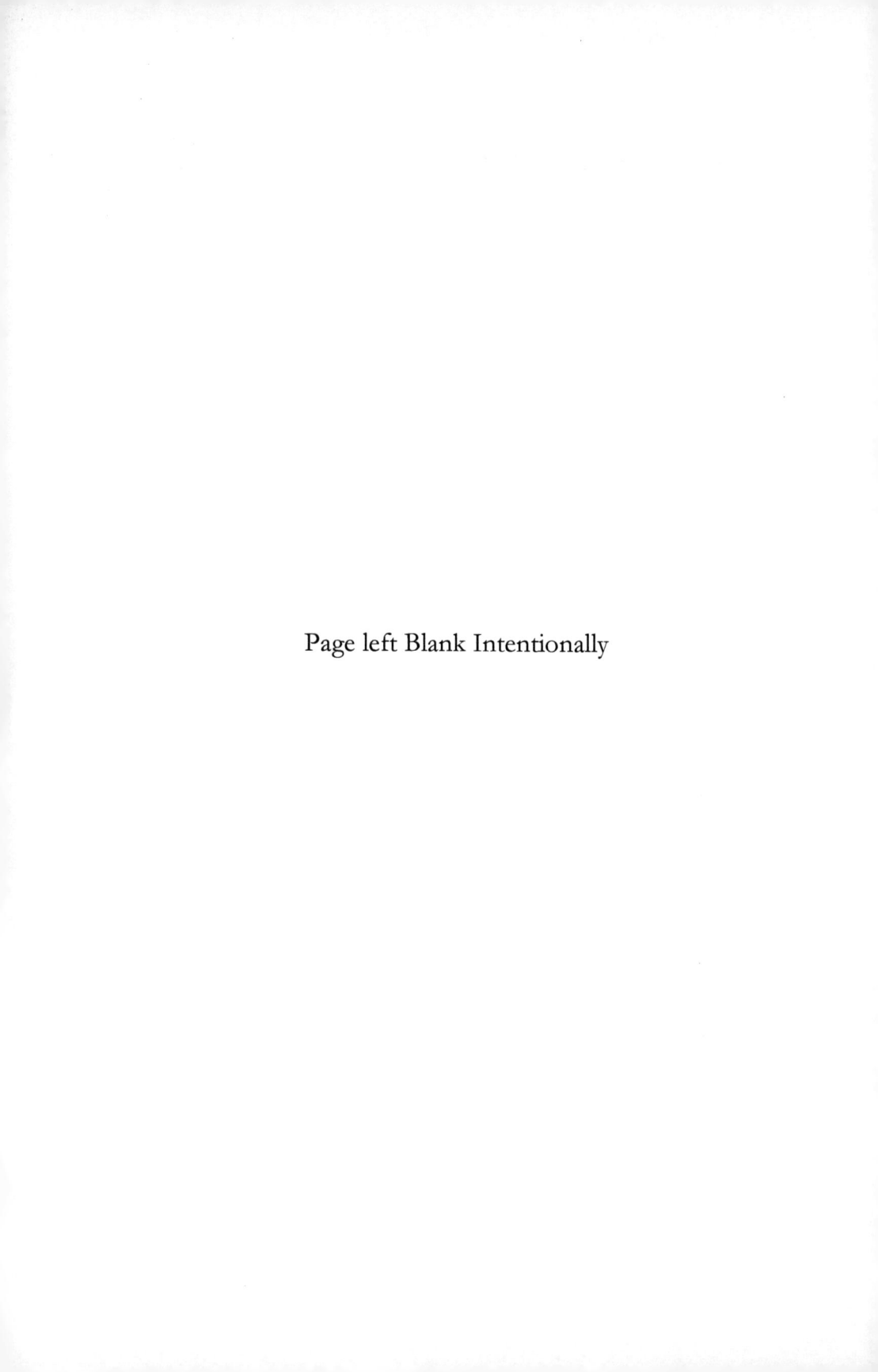

Contents

Dedication i
About The Writer iii
Terminology And Other Nuances As Used In This Write-Up With Intended Meaning: iv
Section 1: Is This A Pre-Face Or A Pre-Farce? 1
Section 2: Agree To These End-To-End Status Book-Ends? 4
Section 3: Only Past Is Ever A Fact, Because It Did Happen 18
Section 4: Most Talk Is Cheap, Most Imagination Is Cheaper 25
Section 5: One Picture May Confuse One More Than 1,000 Words? (Illustrations) 30
Section 6: Prompts Pointing To A Purpose 82
Section 7: When Did We Begin? Are We There Yet? Where Are We Going? 93
Section 8: A Half'S Half-Poke Into The Second Half 104
Section 9: The Odds Of The Two Halves Meeting 113
Section 10: The Two + Two = Four Types Of Big-Bullies 123
Section 11: Consequences & Constancy Of Brain Growth And The Awesome Foursome 135
Section 12: Only "Us" To Remain, Kill All Others 156
Section 13: The Homo-Sapien's Easiest Tasks: Thinking & Saying 192
Section 14: First Set Of Zigzag Migrations With Backtracking 207
Section 15: The Change Of Physique, Chimp To Homo-Sapien 226
Section 16: The Forever Two-Bag Baggage 239
Section 17: Science And Religion – Beyond The Polar Opposites 257
Section 18: Are You A Homo-Sapien Avatar? 274
Section 19: Is There A Better Way To Rid Falsities 283

Section 1: Is this a Pre-Face or a Pre-Farce?

This is just a write-up, - like a minor thesis with some allowable personal subjectivity with humor, - with heavy theorizing about much of the past of homo-sapiens. As far as any facts are considered, **ONLY past can ever be a fact** in this universe because the past did happen, but we may not have the factual records. All future is hallucination, regardless of which clever mouth describes it impressively. The problem with any past is "knowing it accurately, what really happened," while the problem with future is there are too many claimants who seem to know it accurately.

Consider these pre-faces and pre-farces:

- This is a write-up that was cooking up inside this octogenarian's brain which is possessed of some extra dulled capacity, and that dormant region goads him into *anything other than retiring (even if it means trouble);*

- This is not a true story because it couldn't entirely be so with many unclear facts and theories;

- This is not fully fictional either because there may be some or more truths and realities in it;

- This is not good history because many parts lack an accurate accounting of the past;

- This is not a comedy on realities because it includes too many real tragedies downgrading the Greeks;

- This is not fully a mystery because the realities of both the beginning and the end of the write-up are well known as well as agreed upon by both of us; The book-ends are clean and clear;

- This is not a thriller because, in the long-haul real living for most homo-sapiens is not comfortable to be in a constant adventure;

- This is not all-science because *science is too recent* **in relation to eons of faiths, beliefs**, and related art forms for too many homo-sapiens and also science is a less understood methodology;

- This is *not at all* "religion", definitely because it is certainly is expected to be "the anti-so" of faiths, and beliefs;

- There are no major new lessons to be learned because many of us already have had such long experiences in living;

- This is not fully a serious theme, and it has much silly humor built in just to entertain the reader and please the writer;

- If to you, all this is nothing but the writer's braggadocio, you can stop reading after the section on the Illustrations and then decide?

- All in all, this is merely a write-up with ideas cooking inside this octogenarian's brain for decades *about the evolutional steps that resulted in homo-sapiens from chimps*, and hopefully, it is at least a bit amusing and interesting to be worthy of your time, even if it becomes argumentative between both of us fairly quickly.

(Yours humbly and still evolving) **Shreedharaa**

Section 2: Agree to these end-to-end status book-ends?

A supernova is the brightest and most destructive explosion that finally happens to a sufficiently large star. It is often observable by us with the naked eye. It shatters and scatters almost its entire body's elements, while sometimes its remainder turns into a black hole. We still get most of our earthly material as minuscule portions from such explosions, even after many millions of years after the explosion has taken place and contents are spread over 360 deg solid angle.

We are all made of such stars' discards, though we only need just a few of the 100 possible elements and their compounds from the explosions to make up our entire body. Primarily, we need hydrogen, oxygen, and carbon. This stars' discard-collecting has been happening for over four billion years on the grounds we stand on, in the waters we frolic in, and in the wind that blows all over us.

Now, how long do you plan to live and how far back can you go in your mind into the past? Can you go back in time and describe *historically some things that really happened* on this earth? Your answers will be the telltale sign of your thinking and your knowledge of the history of homo-sapiens "**us**".

Do you have any idea when the following things came into existence as "matured realities for us to touch, use, and enjoy?"

Starting with the latest (You definitely know several of these):

- The plethora of intelligent phones with multiple instant media connections and, prior to that, all
- forms of computers that they evolved out of;
- All forms of sound and movie paraphernalia, rotary phones, handheld movie cameras;
- Propeller and turbine-driven airplanes, liquid fuel rockets, with and without microprocessors, - the micro-processors having had their own fascinating evolution;
- Countless varieties of cars and automobiles evolved over the last 160 years, not forgetting the discovery of oil- gushers, kerosene, petrol, and lubricating oils replacing whale fat; Literal extinction of the majestic Moby-Dicks;
- Pristine surgery rooms, hospitals with all kinds of medicines and sickness eradicators, and the use of anesthesia;
- All types of imaging and x-ray machines to look inside messy homo-sapiens like this writer;

- All varieties of "tu-tooing Wabash cannonballs" that ran on steam first, then diesel, or electric.

Somebody had to figure out all those above first, and then figure how to make them, and then keep repairing them! All of the above came about within hardly the last 325 years of this 4,500,000,000-year-old planet we call earth.

Important note!

None of these items mentioned above were ever conceived, written about, or made in the impeding confines of a church, a synagogue, a temple, a mosque, a mandhir (a Hindu place of worship), or some such place of your faith, into which you probably were lovingly "carried in" to visit as often as possible as a child, even before you could crawl or keep your eyes open. Also, none of these "great gadgets", *without which we cannot live anymore*, was ever made inside a royal palace, a political building, a bank, or an insurance company's offices.

Hopefully, this writer is getting somewhere with you.

To what age do you think you will live? Any idea? Just blurt out a number that immediately comes to your mind. Did this writer hear you say, say 90? The writer assures you that today's medical and medicine greats *will not let you die* until you are 90 + 10 = a 100 *at least*.

Let both of us go a little further back in time historically before this write-up starts annoying you. If you are educated and a bit of a curious reader (no matter whatever biased flavors favor your taste), you may be able to say something about the history of shooting rockets into space –going to the moon, to the space explorers to distant planets, the history of of-late jet planes that can create sonic booms, plain propeller planes that came before them, the great-grandkids of steam locomotives, namely today's 300 kmh bullet trains, race cars, and everything else science has to offer. Let us call these as "those on this side".

Then, go over to the faiths and religions of "those on the other side" and compare them both back-to-back. Did the houses of worship encourage, impede, or in any way get involved in all of the items mentioned above? By and by, the houses of worship were a hindrance to the newly emerging engineering offices of inventions and their manufacturing. Note: all these "things of science" mentioned need both, - fuel to energize their workings and skilled homo-sapiens to operate them and keep them running.

There never ever was such an extremely smart *single homo-sapien*, wandering around bipedally on the earth with intense curiously, by just looking at the stars' blown up debris laying at his feet, and then some more of it in the ocean's water surrounding him, and then also staring curiously a bit closer at *the soft dark **black rocks*** lying all around, with probably many other *embedded **shiny rocks*** – occasionally all of them smeared with yucky oozing, somewhat useless-*looking dark oily fluid*…and then in a fit of inspiration he yelled, "Hey guys! I know how to make use of *all this stuff,* put them together to make some great machines that can double or quadruple your fields' grain output, in less than half the time. I can even use this stuff to make rockets that will take you to the moon and bring you back."

That kind of yelling was done by many many smart dudes over several hundred years, once each one of them understood the possibilities in the dirt, rocks shiny or black, and oily goop they were looking at, while each one stood on the shoulders of his predecessors to look farther.

We can keep gradually going back in time like that deeper into history, but let us *simply skip the nearest **past greatest** 532 years (or so).* Then we go backward several hundred years more while passing through the dull years, the so-called Middle Ages. We can go still further back through the years and the exciting times of the Turks, the Arabs, the Romans, the Macedonians, the Greeks, and the Persians.

We can muddle our way further back, arguing constantly about all the murky history through the years of the Assyrians, Mesopotamians, and Egyptians. Since most of homo-sapiens in the west routinely love to neglect the great civilizations of the Indus Valley India, and many developing regions of China, the writer reminds you also to include the years of these two into your knowledge of history. That would probably be it, as far back as most of us, this writer included, will go into ancient times. By now, through these exercises of going back into ancient history, we may have gone back to about 8,000 years and witness the 1st ever graffiti on the cave walls of bison, horse, lion etc. in color... These original cave wall scribblings of creatures, it seems, was done that far back, almost 10, 000 (10k) years ago.

Researchers pour over all the available records in studying such cave paintings in awe. They also studying that period's homo-sapiens' home construction methods, and the hunting/killing tools introduced by them. The writer would like to round this 8000 (8k) to simply as 10k and call that whole 10k period, *throughout this write-up as* **"The Modern Evolutionary Era"** *of homo-sapiens.* The evolutionary 6m years or so that *preceded* the homo-*whatevers* beyond 10k *ends at the beginning* of this Modern Evolutionary Era.

The writer is dealing with the unrecorded 6m years of chimp's evolution to homo-sapiens, followed by The Modern Evolutionary Era of 10k of the homo-sapiens, which is *fairly well* recorded. Here the term homo-*whatever(s)* will be used denote any hominin of any particular species whose specificity and given Latin name is unimportant for this write-up. Anything prior to The Modern Evolutionary Era is generally theorized by dating and studying fossils by researchers. Dating fossils and interpreting them as to the physical structure of a particular homo-*whatever* has become quite advanced. Again, a homo-*whatever* is some hominin that preceded the homo-sapien (i.e., is **us**) at some time in the past, and we are not going to worry about his precise scientific Latin names for this write-up.

The reason we jump-skipped the last ~532 years from today is that, a whole host new gadgets and all sorts of inventions of guns, cannons, and other discoveries involving manufacturing machinery, locomotives etc., were developed by us homo-sapiens during that short period of the few ~ hundreds of years. Such immeasurably useful gadgets like microscopes, telescopes were neither understood nor figured out for numerous thousands of years before those 532 years. We revel at bragging about the history of the last 6,000 years and the beginnings of the Egyptians, and that really is not much to brag about when compared to the inventions of the last few hundred years!

Our bragging does become so dearly important when it comes to whether one is the descendent of the Sumerians, Huns, Greeks, Alexander, Darius, Julius Cesar or Genghis Khan, etc. *and etc.*! When you compare the laziness of their brains in relation to the mental activity of Galileo, Newton, Faraday, James Clerk Maxwell etc., it amounts to no more than picking up their swords, bow and arrows, mount their chariots *and go killing their neighbors.*

But, all those even if truly great homo-sapiens of several thousands of years before the stated 532 years, everywhere, anywhere, —they knew zilch about *how the universe really worked.* Today, we know a lot, even if we do not know all, especially about "the intensely being studied" mysterious items of dark matter, dark energy, and such.

Absolutely no offense is intended in saying this bluntly about the bygone ancient *scholars – none at all.* The writer has great admiration for many greats that went before us for thousands of years. It is those trigger-happy killers he complains about, since the writer comes from a region that touted non-violence for eons.

With full respect and adulation for the brains and hard work of the ancients, the writer still commits to saying they did not know how to figure out, or how our world really worked. Why the true explanations in understanding the universe took so long, and then all clarifications happened so fast in just about 170 years is an enigma to this writer. He would like to theorize the reasons for this late bloom of hominin brains, while he encourages you to do the same. The writer repeats apologetically: it is a statement of fact that what we learned and saw, using extraordinary science and math developed in the last 250 or so years most about this world and the universe. The homo-sapiens of before that time *through into antiquity* understood a very small fraction of the recent findings of the realities of the natural material world.

The writer nevertheless loves history, and adores and loves all those greats of antiquity, though he knows they basically guessed at "things" after using their senses of sight, smell, hearing, and touch, and at the most rudimentary level with no proper assisting mental or material tools (by mental tools, a scientific method is meant, though the brains were ready and available). The most prominent assisting tools they had were physical, useful to kill another for dominance often over their own kind. *They relied on thinking*, and per this writer, *by and large,* **all thinking is fundamentally hallucination** *at the core level,* be it the most harmless routine thinking or the most profound thinking that happens once in thousands of years to particular individuals. *Thinking by itself may relate zero to the real worlds out there.* It is way over-rated.

The teachings of the intensely admired thinking followed by sayings of few of the men eons ago, admired today by homo-sapiens by the billions, was never tested for evidence in the scientific sense to be in agreement to reality. Yet these individuals each convinced millions of converts in short periods during their own times about the efficacy of their sayings. Based on evidence of "the truths" we know today, a good portion of their rhetoric may be *dumped into the dustbin because it has been proved without doubt to be* **simply wrong** *in relation to reality.*

Suffice it to say here that the greatest thinking by homo-sapiens of antiquity, as considered so by millions of homo-sapiens of today that we know of, was all hallucination, and *none of these charismatic thinkers seems to have realized so, - that evidence to what they said is lacking.* Any skeptics who confronted such hallucinators of antiquity by contrarian arguments paid the price with their lives! Consider - To almost everyone even today the sun rises erroneously in east and erroneously sets in west is a testament to their *stubbornness in wrong beliefs.* **The sun in reality does nothing of that sort.** Correctly saying, the sun *appears* in our east and *disappears* in our west every day is more appropriate. It is only a small correction, but many such add up.

Expert researchers of today seem to be able to go back about eight to ten thousand years ago and brag that they can decipher what homo-sapiens during The Evolutionary Modern Era (10k) were up to, with reasonable clarity. They have the tools *today* to study the minutest pieces of evidence left behind by the homo-sapiens in these 10k years.

Coming to an agreement is needed between us. Unless you and this writer have some reasonable agreement on the following words and phrases, the writer may be misinterpreted frequently. *The writer heavily favors everything science explains.*

The words and phrases to be understood in today's sense are and -of the type: evolution, science, scientist, scientific method, scientific evidence, observations, scientific tools such as telescopes and image magnifiers, using more of one's senses and tools *with a bit less thinking, use of scientific languages such as math and graphs, constant questioning of the conclusions of any scientist with no permission ever needed from him,* scientific truth, humanism, abandoning all faith and beliefs in supernaturals. In short, science is the preferred by the writer, *in opposition* to faith, belief, creator, god, **god-etc.**

The damage done through words such as faith, religion, belief, **god-etc.**, and other hallucinated words of similar type from thought alone has been immense indeed and it continues. You are allowed to judge this writer harshly for the above line, but would you please wait till you read this write-up, hopefully to the end? It is a short thesis type write-up.

The writer will not question for a moment the extraordinary creative arts that have flourished through a homo-sapiens' thinking (read = hallucinating) capacity, and justifiably most is credited to faith. However, such creativity that emanates from within but its meaning never is verified against reality and contrarian-ly re-verified to be truly hallucination only through science, - should become gradually outdated and studied in historical context only, - hopefully henceforth so *by everyone.* Such a bold statement should be explored, too.

A new wave of creative arts will evolve which will have no need for religious connotations involving **god-etc.**, since creativity is after all thinking (= hallucinating) before saying or doing anything, and all thinking, being all hallucination at first, is always available to go into myriads of directions with options to be creative again and again. True, there is no such a thing as a new idea that is bad until verification proves it so. On the contrary a reality of nature that is in waiting to be verified by the homo-sapien has no options.

Reality in the universe has no options, thinking has as many options as there are homo-sapiens willing to think.

All the foregoing can be summed up - "***Science and math are the only things that are the same for everybody, everywhere, forever,*** and they both will (should) bring anyone to the same known/declared answer. These words, by and large, cannot be applied to anything in the years **before** the immediate ~300 years of past. We now come to the two ends we both need to agree for you to enjoy reading and critiquing this write-up to your heart's contents. This request needs only to be temporary, and the agreement can be discarded based on your thinking and beliefs. The writer humbly requests you to accept these following notions:

- That homo-sapiens (i.e. us) evolved from apes, specifically bipedal chimps (i.e., in other words clearly, we were not created by any creator or god, however loftily that is described in books / "qitaabs"/ commandments). Some initial chimp with genetic mutation must have initiated preference to two-legged walks and gave up tree dwelling about 6 million years ago. This is the first end for agreement.

- Only homo-sapiens (i.e. us) existed at the start of The Modern Revolutionary Era (i.e., 10 k years ago). This is the second end to for agreement. (This second end is a fact, known to us from to the conquest of all lands and seas by the adventurous conquistadors with their superior tools against everybody they faced, ~532 years ago.)

- Some other minor points to agree on:

- The first biped (i.e., a chimp walking on hind legs) started somewhere in the middle of the African continent, in or near the regions of Chad. For this, we will agree with the expert researchers of today who say so, unless you know something better.

All else are totally fascinating changes that happened within those 6 million years. They are to be theorized by the writer; you are eagerly encouraged to theorize too, and this writer will figure out a way to publish your counter ideas directly in the main print (i.e., not as a footnote) after evaluation by chosen unbiased editors and with your permission. **_Look to the back cover._** For anything else we will rely on experts' fossil studies as and when we need. So many interesting changes have taken place in "**us**" who started as bipedal chimps and ended as homo-sapiens, throughout the 6 million years or so, since the first bipeds in Chad!

Section 3: ONLY Past is Ever a Fact, because it did Happen

Whether we know what happened accurately or not, *past acts are the only facts* in this universe, because they did happen.

Thinking of the future and hoping, etc., are simply hallucinations. Most of the time in today's living such hallucinations are extremely mild and one is not aware that that is what they are, but hallucinations they still are. "*I think* I will bear the discomfort and go to the bathroom only after reaching home" (one may not bear the discomfort enroute and find a place "to go" proving that the original thought was just a hallucination and the final act was different), - likewise "I should get that call any minute now *(I think)*" "I should start preparing for my talk *(I think)*". The preceding were all hallucinations because the thinking may not involve any muscular movement of any part of "the body", as of yet and the thoughts may or may not be fulfilled as thought, making them mild form of hallucinations. Repeating for emphasis: all pure thinking is pure hallucination that happens in region 3 of the brain only (see illustration 13)

"*I think* the CEO should announce the personnel cuts tomorrow morning and not wait till Friday" is a much weightier hallucination if one is only thinking. Only if some muscular movement takes place of the thought, even if as simple as those requiring oral sounds, then the hallucination from region 3 has been acted upon by regions 1 and 2, see Illustration 13. The more we study past facts accurately, if at all possible, the more we will know how homo-sapiens will hallucinate for their future behavior. In today's digital world, accurate record keeping *forever* is possible in most minimal space, because of digitization.

Someday each one living will die and there is nothing after that but for the dust and ashes of one's body's material mingling back into the dirt of the earth. It mingles with the earth's materials to form the future complex primordial soup and then into a large number of new eggs and sperms, of which less than a handful continue with new lives. Most of one's body remains in the earth to fuel other living bodies in due course. Knowing this disappointing truth, **full living must be the top priority of every homo-sapien while being alive**. With today's tools it is a cinch to permanently store all the memorabilia about anyone and anyone's pets too in digitized form "in multiple copies" in a billionth space needed to bury a casket. It can include their vocals too! Wouldn't you love to hear the voice of Abe Lincoln, and many other near and dear to you, and may be more of your favorite entertainers? To the amazement of this writer 60 years ago it was a cinch to go the library and borrow vinyl that had voices of Kennedy, Roosevelt and other presidents. Today you can have digitized versions of everybody and their anything.

Since the existing beliefs in the supernatural (**god-etc.**) for thousands of years have enriched homo-sapiens with extraordinary art, culture, music, etc., in future after adopting a changed culture by completely removing any beliefs in the **god-etc.**, the new aura of scientific thinking will gently create a different type aura of art and culture in due course, just as beautiful as it was in the old.

New reasoning dictates there should be no violence-based actions in future resulting in killings, *but for legitimate self-defense*; Study the awesome powers nature has in all sorts of *its* explosions. This puny homo-sapien should be ashamed that he thinks that power can be mastered against homo-sapiens he does not approve of. Yes he can but only temporarily since the brain growth shows no signs of stopping and soon enough his one-upmanship will be challenged by the new. Figure out the use of nature's powers for peaceful purposes and *common benefits for all homo-sapiens and the environment.*

No one has ever proved anything about any living thing after its death. **No one has ever come back after dying, and assuredly no one ever will**. We have to swallow this truth. Let us not chase after a soul after death because 'there ain't none'. The random destruction and distribution of body's material after death, consumption of it in a cyclical manner by other creatures, is visually obvious. That one particular creature, namely "us", has the desire and capacity to think and hallucinate anything is the root cause of myths about myriads of apparitions of the dead reappearing. Such thinking can only be attributed to hallucination. No other creature suffers from this conflict about the dead.

Even if one argues that it is the soul that survives and enters another body, then answer to Kipling's questionnaires, What (soul)! Who, when, why, where, how? Answer: **there is no such a thing as a soul after death**, and hence nothing of that sort can enter any living thing. While for the living, the deep emotional capabilities and intertwining of memories due to region 3, can make one feel "a homo-sapien" has soul, **while the individual is alive**, and that is OK.

We know in detail how another body forms from a randomly winning sperm (half homo-sapien = half soul?) meeting a randomly waiting egg (half homo-sapien=the other half soul?). Surely one cannot think through a soul of a dead homo-sapien becoming two half souls, hanging around to mingle again to enter as half-s a male and a female wanting to do **IT** with the blending of the two half souls! You see the problem here for the 'Rubber Souls' so flexible and compliant?

So, into which half, where, and when, and how, and why does the soul enter? Are there rules of the two half souls becoming a full soul? Is every competing sperm carrying a half soul? Is every egg in waiting dormant also is carrying half souls? Or the chosen half souls are waiting separately or as one to enter at the instant of conception? You see, once one has the freedom to think and say, any outcome can be said-through. But reality must be explained using science.

The process immediately following conception is complex enough and what are the rules for soul formation? Does the soul also come in halves (Rudyard's 6 friends may not help us now)? Does the soul in a living life at death divide self to go in half and half into a new sperm and egg, and become whole at the inception of conception? So many soul-searching questions! The ancients had the easier task of just thinking and saying whatever they wished to think and say, cleverly of course.

You see, conceptualizing a happening (= thinking, hallucinating) first cannot mean its physicality in nature can be described later. **The process needs to be reversed.** Knowing the physicality fully or partially, the conceptualization of a process for explanations should be formulated *then after*. The complex feeling of soul's existence is another hallucinated emotional item region 3 accommodates *while living,* for full satisfaction of the homo-sapien. All in all, this writer feels that a soul is simply an imaginary entity for the living homo-sapien *only*. The nourishment items left behind in tombs, crypts, and within monuments for the dead homo-sapien have never been touched or disturbed by the dead homo-sapien. **Doesn't anyone ever get what the lessons are** *even after hundreds upon hundreds of years of observation?* Does the ego and fears of death have to be satisfied **to that extent of silliness**? – and then we are forced to admire that? Baah-humbug.

A securely placed dead body never moves even a nano-micro-millimeter, while a living body can walk a 1000 miles multiple times in a lifetime. Yet homo-sapiens like to be duped into admiring mummies through the propagated ideas of influential historians! Why? *What is the reason for this hypocritical behavior* that the homo-sapiens of the past behaved so stupidly? Why not call "*a spade the spade*" and dig out all this hypocritical dirt within us? Is it not just a big show-off of the famous and falsely educated, falsely influenced homo-sapiens to teach such history that silliness should be glorified?

Maybe the desire, hope in an imaginary afterlife, or the fear of dying creates this staunch atmosphere of false belief. The big brain in cahoots with a few influential faith-based homo-sapiens is the root cause of this false belief system. Fortunately, the big brain can also cure this false belief system by training us to live as fully as possible with nature and reason, and observe history with proper perspective of forgiveness towards the ignorance laden of false "souls" living on false ideas of faith. Think of all the tribes, cultures, and languages simply and stupidly destroyed by the so-called superior homo-sapiens to the point of complete elimination *and now (today) feeling bad about such actions of the ancestors.* **The writer loves the Region 3 of brain creating such conflicts!** It is one of the saddest periods on the past history of the big-bullies from the west: - they destroyed native Americans everywhere *on two continents that together are much larger than Europe plus all of Russia put together*, the culture and languages of the natives is almost no more *in reality.*

Uyyay-yayyay-yay (the reader is supposed to look down and shake the head left to right every time he says the words over and over)

Whose fault it is, is not important; but the realization that *homo-sapiens will do killing needlessly is, because long ago they chose the wrong tine on the fork of brain's options, the tine that only enhanced the violent tendencies inherited from chimps.*

Now we have come to the super capabilities of AI where no language and its sounds, or its culture needs to go extinct ever, even if some misguided homo-sapiens of future succeeds in eliminating others they don't like.

Section 4: Most Talk is Cheap, Most Imagination is Cheaper

No one detects what one is imagining internally, and hence it is a cheap way to hide a homo-sapien's hallucinations. One may not prefer to listen to the talker because there is no assurance that the talk matches what the homo-sapien's internal intent is honestly. Hence talk can be cheap also, sometimes it being pure lies. This is the normalcy among homo-sapiens generally. On the other hand, still, millions of homo-sapiens are duped each and every moment by talkers whose prejudices fit their own biases but they have realized that homo-sapiens can be very easily lied to.

Without becoming an educated global citizen with compassion deep inside, a homo-sapien will always carry deeply buried false prejudices that can be baseless. Sadly, most homo-sapiens who get their ***real education*** only after age 6 in accredited secular schools use their need for education only to find a well-paying job, but not to become global citizens with some compassion.

Can you show me a diploma of yours showing your detailed training from 0 to 6 years? Does it sound like an unintelligible silly request? The writer bets ***no one***, let alone you, can put together a small 3-page resume describing your life in those years of intense training from your birth to 6 years as your diploma. Yet it is a very important "first document", though nobody will ask for it, you should be able to show it in your own mind, *for the understanding of self* and for your future development without conflicts.

Everyone who has gone to some type of secular school starting at age 6, can show all sorts of diplomas from their schools and colleges, in the form of certificates, degrees, employment records, - for scores of years *from age 6. But when the homo-sapien dies, he is permanently remembered on some sort of a graveyard stone, or a symbolized plaque or paper, what was decided for him already in his zero to the 6th year!* Almost nothing of what he was for the following 75+ years counts! **What kind of hypocrisy is this?** But for today's digitizing availabilities only since a few years, all his life can be mostly forgotten in a matter of a few years.

We come across kids of tender age who are trained to recite passages verbatim from, their caretakers' chosen book of faith (qitaab, pusthak, commandments). False knowledge it is, most of it, and it was wrongfully thrust on them.

The extra-large growing brain can be activated into high gear very quickly right from infancy, based on the training at home *and the surroundings* and activities that a child goes through. The homo-sapien brain is constantly growing in size with every generation imperceptibly, too small to observe even in 100 lifetimes. As an example, a particular individual though with average or below average brain size may have descended from a long line of readers, leaders, thinkers, and observers of nature or art. If this individual somehow got exposed to new unknown phenomenon in the universe that excites him, his brain, though not of exceptional quality or size, *is ripe in preparation* to absorb any phenomenon for further investigations.

His creative nature though having a smaller than average brain might still simply explode into new territories for deeper investigations! **The point:** One does not have to have a large brain to explode into creativity. Darwin, James C Maxwell are definitely great example who had had such effects on their selves, and there are so many others, but *such explosion of talent only happens on the science side*. Explosion of new talent on faith side is no longer possible because supernaturalism has been proved to be false, and a dead end.

Keeping morals and ethics aside, both of which can be perfectly taught independently of faith-based education, It appears good morals and ethics *preceded the preachers of faith* well before they dreamt-up the concepts of **god-etc.**

Pseudo religious to serious religious concepts, along with rituals and chants must have started well before The Modern Evolutionary Era, may be by 5k years before, which means 15k years ago from today. Such concepts must have been in a very rudimentary form with the 1st holy man, Illustration 7. These deep-rooted concepts will not be eradicated from the homo-sapiens' brain even in a hundred years time, but perhaps in 200 years or so with persistent science-based education.

We need enough caretakers (parents) who are going to be responsible to the birth of their new homo-sapiens to thoroughly understand **at their own core levels**, that there never was or ever will be anything supernatural that will affect the living *of their own or their future infants' lives*. - but for morals and ethics common to most homo-sapiens, all the supernatural "stuff" of any holy book (qitaab, pusthak, commandments) must be discarded. In more words, a newborn should learn right from start *in the most suitable way* that all creation universally is by nature and creature inclusive of homo-sapiens.

Once these new young ones so correctly trained, as they grow older, have offsprings of their own, - they will be in an easier position to raise their new offsprings in the most correct humanistic nature's way. Mind you! We need to develop these secular ideas across borders, cultures, religions, ethnicities, languages, and races, **without ever impinging on the cherished identities of any community.**

A lot of new culture in science, arts, music, drama must be given the opportunity to germinate in the culture of the new homo-sapiens who agree to refuse to teach their offspring anything supernatural.

The muscular big-bullies and the super-egotistical hallucinating scribes really messed up the concept of full living for simple homo-sapiens. Full living entails the full study of the universe for the benefit of homo-sapien and other living. It never calls for muscular or any other type of big-bulliness.

Section 5: One Picture may Confuse one more than 1,000 Words? (Illustrations)

```
Illustration - 1, drawn to scale
```

400 — Earliest already Bipedal (chimp) 6.0 to 5.4 mya — 1
483 — 5.6/4.9 mya — 2
586 — 5.1/4.5 mya — 3
649 — 4.6/4 mya — 4
732 — 4.2/3.6 mya — 5
816 — 3.7/3.1 mya — 6
900 — 3.3/2.6 mya — 7
983 — 2.8/2.2 mya — 8
1066 — 2.4/1.8 mya — 9
1149 — 2/1.3 mya — 10
1233 — 1.5/.9 mya — 11
1317 — 1/.4 mya — 12
1400 — Today's Homo-sapien — 13

Typical brain size in CCs based on uniform growth

typ ~ 0.46 m years span

50 000 years into future ~ 1483 cc

Brain size growth
mya = million years ago
cc = cubic centimeters

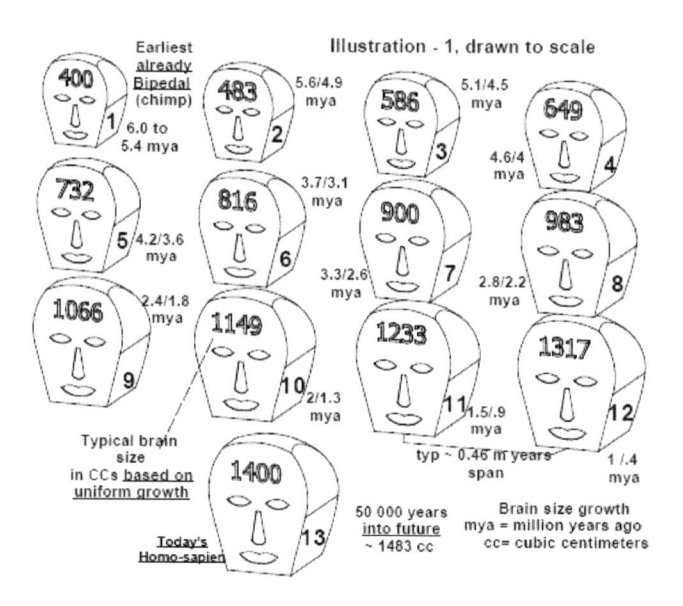

Illustration 1: This illustration shows the fact that the small 400 cubic centimeter brain of a chimp, which had just become a biped about 6 million years ago, evolved into the 1,400 cubic centimeter powerhouse of today's homo-sapien. The chimps that did not become bipeds stayed as chimps and evolved in their own way to today's chimps. For us homo-sapiens back then it was a tiny 400 cc brain. Now? We have a massive 1,400 cc brain on the average. That is an increase of 350%. The 400 cc of 6 mya is a figure that is assumed to be based on present-day

chimps and any fossils of chimps going back 6 to 7 million years.

In this write-up, we will assume the growth to have been a uniform growth from 400 cc to 1,400 cc. No one can yet (or maybe ever) say if the growth was along some curve or in spurts. For the basis of why the brain grew, the writer makes the assumption that a genetic mutation was introduced in some particular newborn chimp. An extraordinary mutation indeed it must have been, because if it is true, never has there been such a mutation introduced in the history of the earth to any other creature.

Every *half*-million years, the brain gained just 84 cc. Simple math! Break that down further and we get: 0.0167 cc every century or about in four homo-sapien generations. And here's the kicker—in all likelihood, the homo-sapien brain is still growing with each succeeding generation, *on the average*. Why would the brain growth stop? There's no reason to think it would. The experts may try to chart out a curve to find fluctuations over time, but forget that for this write-up. Assume the rate has been steady *and is relentless*. The brain has been expanding for 6 to 7 million years, and there's no sign that the process has ended. Did the chimp become bipedal gradually or very quickly? This is answered elsewhere.

Illustration - 2

Showing how bipedal and early hominin-groups could have zigzagged and backtracked for 1st 3 million years or more

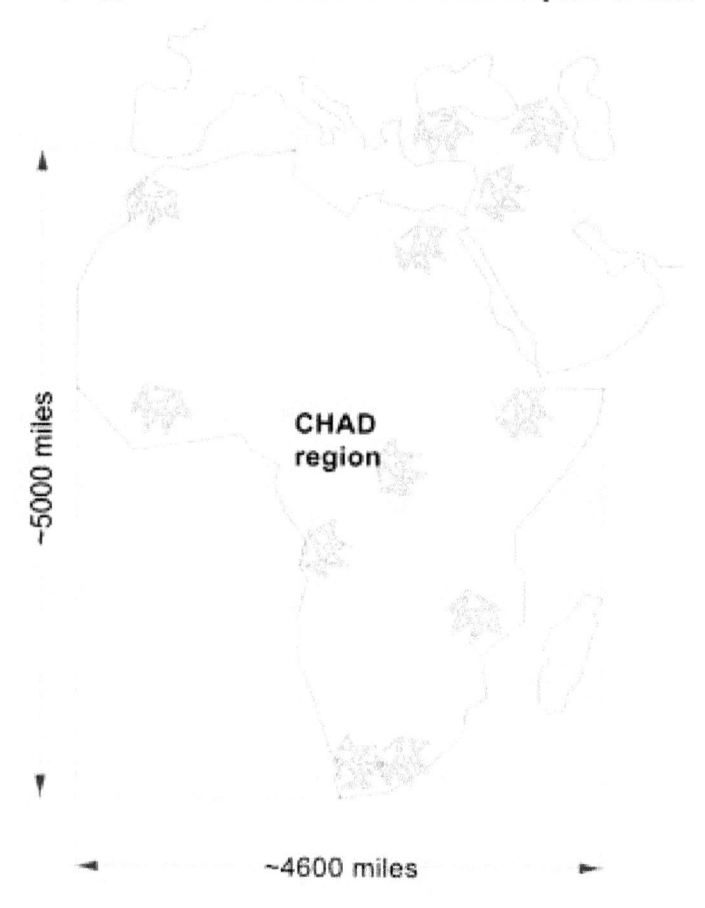

~5000 miles

CHAD region

~4600 miles

Illustration 2: What could be the farthest distances these early wandering bipeds reached, In two or three million years of aimless walking around in Africa? Sinai is the only way out of Africa for them. That's the only escape route into the rest of the earth's lands. There is no other. You might ask, did the bipeds reach the Sinai corridor in half a million years of wanderings? Or at some other random time, maybe in 200,000 years? Fair question. But the writer has made some calculations. He estimates that in two million years, the whole of Africa would have been fully covered on foot as long as the bipeds did not venture across Sinai and zigzagged in all possible directions. The calculations are laid out elsewhere to follow.

Once, any group stumbled across the Sinai passage, they could have ventured beyond over the deserts into the regions that we now call the Levant, the Caucasus, the Anatolia, the Persia, the Arabia, and so on. *It is conceivable that the Sinai was not always a desert* the entire 6m years. Half the time of the two million years may also be enough to make this passage through Sinai to happen. Why? Because Chad, the agreed-upon origin point for the earliest biped, is about a bit north of the halfway mid region across Africa. Maybe, such long time ago the Sinai was lush with vegetation when the bipeds reached it. If it became desert after the bipeds crossed it, then a return journey back into Africa might have been discouraging.

These wanderers wouldn't have moved in straight radial lines for long distances. They would not know anything more than 5 to 10 miles away in any direction. They must have zigzagged, backtracked, and wandered in approximately within a circular region *for many generations constantly in-breeding.* They had no knowledge of direction! No maps. Only instincts—food, safety, survival and sex. For a long time, they still had chimp brains. Basic survival ruled their decisions. Of course, each group must have had the normal muscular big-bully with his harem. New bullies emerged constantly, and the groups must have separated a bit away from each other after several generations, with no two groups having close encounters probably for hundreds upon hundreds of years.

These emerging groups, instinctively preferring to spend nights on land, wouldn't have crossed even shallow rivers because that is not a chimp group's temperament. There are so many large deserts all across Africa; impassable for sure for chimp groups. How about large bodies of water, such as lakes, rivers and oceans? Crossing those being out of the question, it would be interesting to theorize if groups backtracked inland a lot more versus traveled along Africa's long ocean border.

Unlike other continents, Africa doesn't have tall mountain chains as barriers that would have slowed the wanderings of the bipedal groups. The equator cuts right through the middle. No major obstacles to stop these early groups except for predators and competition among groups. None of them would have crossed the Mediterranean to reach Gibraltar or ventured across the Red Sea into southern Arabia. So, from Africa, both regions were out of their reach by direct routing for almost the entire 6 million years until someone invented a boat. Here's the real puzzle: how much zigzagging and backtracking happened before they even began moving away from Chad, and why? What would make them abandon familiar grounds but for them being different than the tree dwellers? Why would the biped chimps leave areas they had settled into for generations? Were they rejected by the tree dweller chimps?

The ace predator, the homo-sapien, would not come into being for several million years (at least 5.5 m years). *The brains of the bipeds were constantly growing*, even if their ability to climb trees was never lost for millennia. Was there constant class warfare by the bipeds on ground with the somewhat inferior chimps in the trees whose brains stayed the same size? Chimps still exist even today, and hence, eliminating them was not a part of the temperament of the bipeds. The writer thinks very soon the primary quarrels of the bipeds evolving with larger brains were *with their own kind in unique ways*. Probably no two groups colonizing some distant regional parts for generations would have exactly the same brain growth size rate which means the same brain sizes after 100s of thousands of years.

(Did you hear about the sexy flirting *biped female chimp* from ground wanting some instant sex climbed up the tree and asked a tree-dweller male chimp, "Hey handsome, want to do **IT** with me, now at this very minute? I am as ready as can be, *just for you.*" The male chimp in the tree replied, "Naah, your butt is not sexy red or blown big and pretty to my liking. My mom would not approve of doing **IT** with you ground-gal anyway."

Soooooo, apparently, noticeable physical changes were already

showing up in the bipeds!) Africa's distances are vast. These groups could have been stuck in the same general area for hundreds of thousands of years. New generations would be born and live out their lives in a single locality. And when they finally crossed paths with distant cousins from far away they wouldn't have had a clue that they were relatives. No way to know they shared ancestors from long ago.

(Note: Any "doing **IT**", in reality for any living creature is incestual, albeit mildly, and with a very long generational gap.)

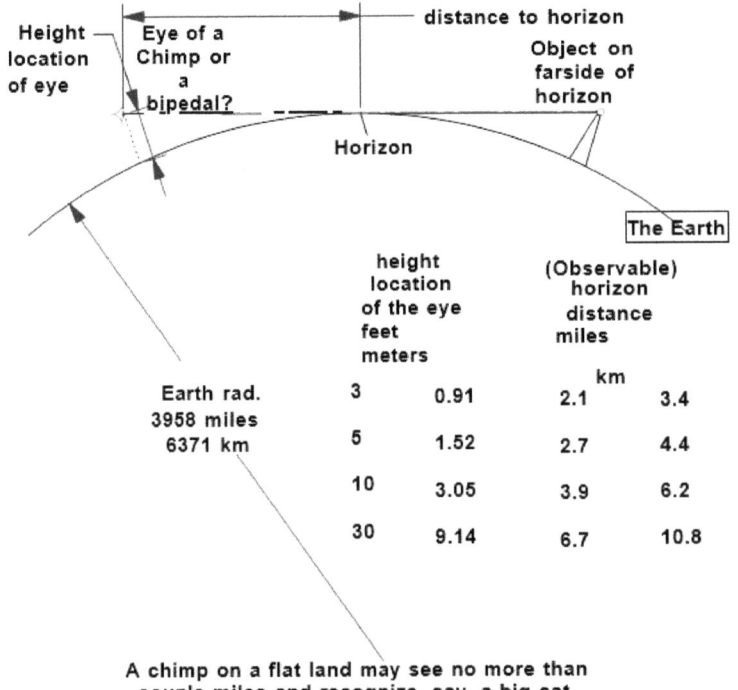

```
                          distance to horizon
Height    Eye of a     |←――――――――――――→|
location  Chimp or                    Object on
of eye      a                         farside of
         bipedal?                     horizon
                      Horizon

                                        The Earth

              height         (Observable)
              location         horizon
              of the eye      distance
              feet             miles
              meters
                                      km
Earth rad.    3      0.91     2.1     3.4
3958 miles
6371 km       5      1.52     2.7     4.4

              10     3.05     3.9     6.2

              30     9.14     6.7    10.8
```

A chimp on a flat land may see no more than
couple miles and recognize, say, a big cat.
Even if a chimp is on a mound or tall tree,
its vision clarity may be limited to say 2
miles
(The picture is not to scale)

Illustration - 3

Illustration 3: It shows the earth's curvature and how far anyone "with very good vision" can see into the horizon when standing on flat land or near the ocean. (The earth is a nice round ball, with a diameter of ~ 8,000 miles and a circumference of ~25,000 miles, roughly.) A chimp, standing 3 feet tall, can see about a mile if its eyesight even allows it to see clearly that far. Doubtful! A 5-foot-tall biped can see a mile and a half, at most.

Place an observer in a 30-foot tree. He-or-she can spot an object of the same height of 30 feet on the other side of the horizon. The distance between them would be 6.7 miles. By geometry, that's how far he-or-she can see when nothing is blocking the view. Anything shorter will be blocked by the curvature of the earth at the horizon. May be, an eagle can see a large cat from that distance, but you or this writer will need binoculars to see even a large elephant on a 30-foot hill beyond the horizon at about 7 miles away.

In normal conditions, on a short grassy prairie, a large predator like a lion could be seen from ¾ of a mile away by a biped with its normal vision. That kind of visibility could mean the difference between survival and death, seeing the danger before it can strike.

Even climbing a tree may not have been a safe solution for a biped because, as shown in many jungle-based incidents, large cats, including lions, seem to easily climb trees to catch a primate, though their heaviness limits how far up a feeble branch the predator can go.

So, why did the chimp take to bipedalism when there is plenty of danger on the ground and plenty enough in the trees too? The writer concludes the biped cannot help it because its normal stance is now to be constantly on twos.

Illustration - 4

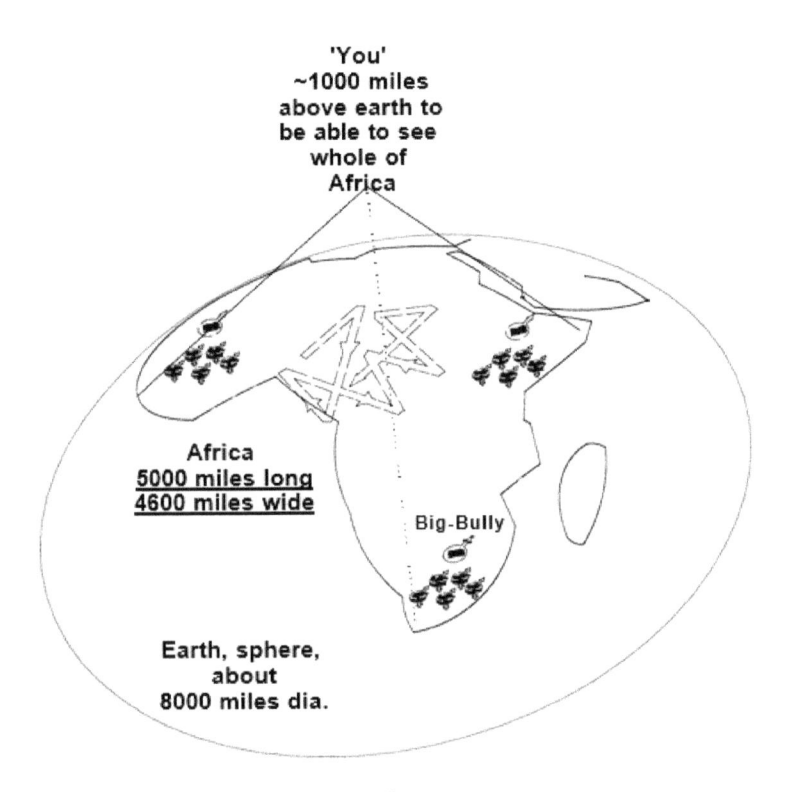

'You'
~1000 miles above earth to be able to see whole of Africa

Africa
<u>5000 miles long</u>
<u>4600 miles wide</u>

Big-Bully

Earth, sphere, about 8000 miles dia.

bipedal homo-*whatever* groups separated by thousands of miles apart, shown for contrast and their descendants may evolve similarly
BUT
separately for 100,000 years or more!!

Illustration 4: This illustration shows Africa as a curved continent on the earth's curvature. The earth's diameter is roughly 8,000 miles. To see the full outline of *all the events* on the African continent for all the 6m years concurrently, you'd need become a super homo-sapien, go ~1,000 miles up into space to a vantage location. Anything less, and some of the edges of Africa will be blocked out of your view. Sophisticated cameras and telescopes would be required by you to zoom in and see details on the African continent *anywhere* to note the movements and behaviors of these wandering bipeds, the homo-*whatever* groups across Africa.

Let's be clear: every wandering group likely had its own muscular big-bully in charge, controlling everything within his group. So, you would see only full groups zigzagging and backtracking whenever the big-bully decided to do so.

Now, when two bipedal groups crossed paths, what happened? If they had evolved away from being chimps into being bipeds for long enough time, they must have resorted to violence through their evolutionary temperamental changes – such actions being brutal and immediate, **with a new kill-them-all attitude** (except, spare the women, of course). This is the writer's view that the new kill your own kind for dominance is strictly a homo-sapien (only) attitude. The stronger group, led by its big-bully, stole everything – food, territory, and women. The writer argues this wasn't just random skirmishing. These battles were savage, probably worse than what the conquistadors did start about 532 years ago when they ravaged the Americas. Why? Because the growing brain had evolved many new emotions *most of* *them inherited bad attitudes* of the chimps much enhanced now and some brand-new bad attitudes, —anger, distrust, vengeance, jealousy, hate, racism, and definitely a liking for killing its own kind into elimination or enslaving. The tree dwelling chimp or any other creature never had such "kill them all" emotions. **This constant barbaric bloodshed into elimination likely explains why only homo-sapiens survived finally.**

The writer is convinced that other homo-whatevers that roamed the earth eons before The Modern Evolutionary Era didn't just vanish, *or like some others would like to say euphemistically, "went extinct."* They were hunted down, killed and eradicated from existence. The writer does not buy into the idea that any of them went extinct naturally. Once chimps started walking upright and their brains doubled to around 800 cc, they must have been smart enough to dominate all other creatures on the earth, as a general rule. But the greed of domination within their own species? That's a new and different story. The weaker bipedal groups (weaker due to a variety of reasons) couldn't stand a chance when it came to competing for food, territory, or women against the more advanced and newer ruthless homo-*whatevers*. *There must have been constant "kill-them-all" fights all over Africa* and new territories beyond Sinai. No two biped groups must have been ever equal, even with similar killing tools. Such differences in groups and its exploitation exists to this day.

So, if you possessed an extended life for millions of years and had the ability to stay 1,000 miles up in space over Africa for about 6 million years, you would see all the zigzagging, backtracking **and killing** of thousands of evolving groups of bipeds, into the finality of the last homo-*whatevers* probably being decimated by the homo-sapiens, *all the while everyone's brains were getting larger, albeit maybe at slightly different rates.* You would have seen a lot of barbaric attacks repeated over and over again. Added to the ever-increasing sexual behavior by homo-*whatevers* within a group, you would see the ever-increasing killing of one group's members by another group's members when two groups encounter each other, with stealing women for sex being a major reason. This is a new form of violence that the evolving homo-*whatevers* acquired as a means to satisfy what has been circulating in their growing brains. No creature goes about killing other creatures with the idea of exterminating others, but the homo-*whatevers* behaved so every time.

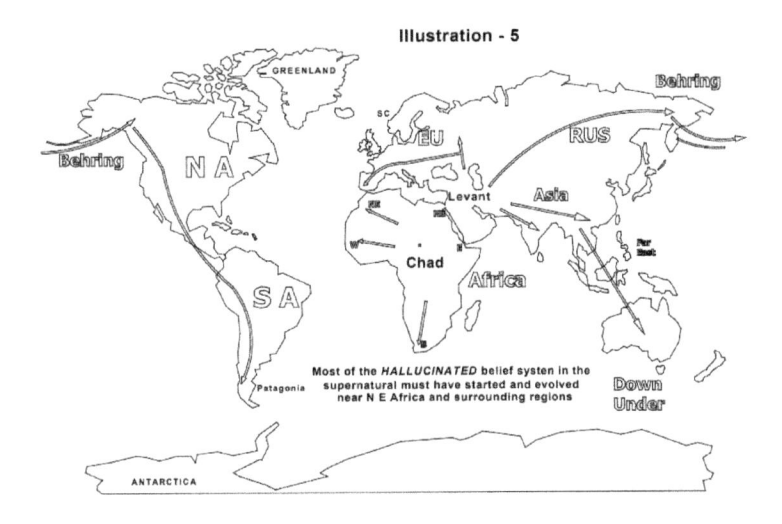

Illustration 5: This illustration shows how the early bipedal homo-whatevers zigzagged and backtracked locally first and then moved across Africa for several million years. Slow, aimless, and repetitive, with the same desires: food within arm's reach, sex with as many females as possible, especially for the muscular big-bully, and personal territory as determined by the big-bully.

Long periods of wandering in haphazard directions, backtracking, and local migrations must always have been influenced by the unobservable influence of the growing brain of each biped, as well as distinct changes in the face, body, skin-eye-hair colors of the new homo-*whatever*, *with* new sounding languages, - simply more things to dislike by the different other homo-*whatevers*. The original bipeds that likely started in what's now Chad and spread to all corners of Africa after couple million years. They could reach without any knowledge of their absolute positions, or others" locations, that they are going to encounter the oceans on several treks.

Why did they move on? Several reasons. Maybe stronger groups forced them out. Maybe they couldn't feed their growing numbers. Maybe they just walked away, looking for safety—nearer to trees or caves that offered shelter. Or they followed their prey, chasing it into new territories. Remember, at the start, these bipeds were not fully herbivorous, but had no predatory instinct to eat meat. *Not yet.* That came later after some stage of their brain growth after they fully embraced walking on two legs in those vast, grassy prairies.

It is possible these hairy, ape-faced homo-whatevers eventually migrated far beyond Africa without knowing they were leaving a continent. Why? Warmer climates; food availability, no competition as long as they did not backtrack; easy access through land bridges in low-lying ocean areas. But they wouldn't have dared venture into the colder regions in the north *for quite some time.* Hence north regions of Europe to east or west, North regions of Russia, Mongolia, China *can be considered as far of lands* just like Americas and Down Under. They must have been still too primitive for long distances combined with cold climates. These creatures were still too close to their chimp roots to survive in such harsh conditions. Since no biped could be an island by itself, none ventured by itself as an adventurer to the vast regions of the north west (Germanic now) into Europe or North East into Asia.

Illustration - 6

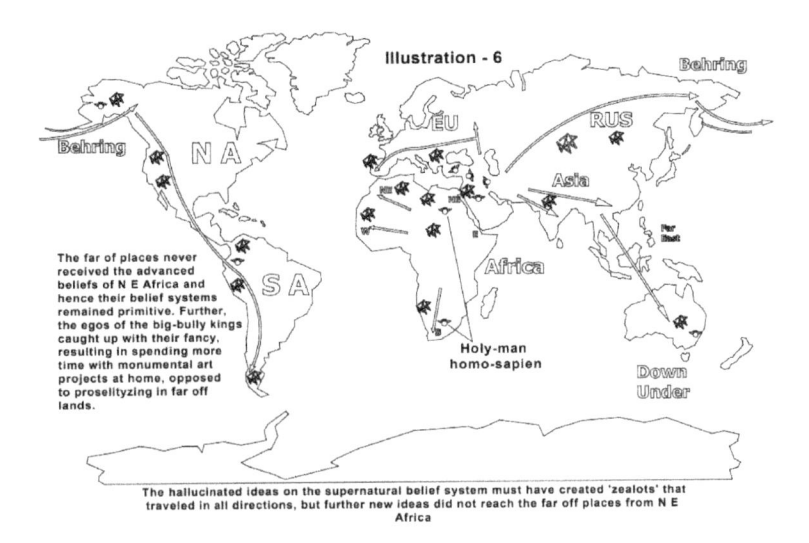

The far of places never received the advanced beliefs of N E Africa and hence their belief systems remained primitive. Further, the egos of the big-bully kings caught up with their fancy, resulting in spending more time with monumental art projects at home, opposed to proselityzing in far off lands.

Holy-man homo-sapien

The hallucinated ideas on the supernatural belief system must have created 'zealots' that traveled in all directions, but further new ideas did not reach the far off places from N E Africa

Illustration 6: This illustration repeats the same migratory zigzagging and backtracking paths of the various homo-whatever species of illustration 5. *But at this stage, something new had emerged giving a tremendous zeal to their travels:*

- Belief systems emerged in at least one of the groups as a start, the new belief being "maybe" "there is life after death."

- Orally expressed language sufficient to communicate new beliefs and new feelings to the commoners.

- Rudimentary ideas of **god-etc**.

This mental shift must have been a welcomed monumental change in the mundane living of homo-*whatevers,* especially in the treatment of the females as sex objects by the crude dominant males. Perhaps all this began abruptly but slowly around 10, 000 to 5, 000 years ago before The Evolutionary Modern Era. For once, the zigzag wanderings of eons may have turned into intensely deliberate movements by the initiators of the new belief systems. Instead of aimless backtrackings, migrations could have become programmed long-distant conquests. These zealots must have been convinced they held the ultimate truths, - trained as missionaries they moved in multiple directions, and spread their beliefs not fearing death and hoping for afterlife in "heaven, paradise".

They must have been 10 times more zealous than the conquistadors of 532 years ago and had the "oomph" to go all over the earth. If you didn't agree with them, you were dead. If you were of slightly inferior homo-whatever status, you probably were killed outright. No debate. No discussion. *This continued brutal, systematic elimination may explain why only homo-sapiens remained as we discovered from 532 years ago, spreading* **all across** *the earth.* It explains why all homo-sapiens everywhere, from the Levant to far-out distant lands and islands, possessed hallucinated rituals in varying degrees with some form of belief in the supernatural. These ideas were cooked up in the abnormally enlarged brain looking for something *to think* and to do, starting originally *probably* in the N E African regions. One thing is for sure! Homo-whatevers started using their brains as thinking mechanisms *as opposed to evidence seeking tools with curiosity.* The zeal of proselytizing also explains why belief systems in more remote areas, in relation to the Levant/Caucasus regions, remained more primitive compared to the constantly evolving advanced philosophies recorded in places like northeast Africa, Anatolia, the Caucasus, and the Levant.

These original advanced regions with *indoctrinated original believers*, didn't just have superior ideas, but they had a lot more, they must have had superior killing machines: metal swords, chariots, horses, and better tools of communication, such as advanced written languages. Their domination in technology before "The Evolutionary Modern Era" made their continued domination inevitable.

Make no mistake—this writer isn't suggesting that the above stated conquering belief systems were better; often, the truth was far from it. They were all fake because they created the never-existent supernatural "stuff". *They were crueler.*

Their power lay in their ability to kill more efficiently, and not necessarily with any moral superiority. That's the ugly truth of their *deviating to the wrong tine of the fork* in the use of their large brains! They preferred the tine of muscular big-bulliness, while a large group in east in the Indian sub-continent unwittingly chose the other tine, the tine of non-violence and pacifistic traits. It is the tine that led to the pacifistic, accommodating philosophies of the Indian sub-continent (albeit with occasional violations). Study the 3 major religions from this region. One will not see any barbaric killing fields here.

At some stage of migrations, interspersed within each group, along with the muscular big-bully, we have the very first newly arrived "bully-pulpit" *holy-homo-sapien* going about creating his own type of belief systems. His charismatic and convincing oratory must have mentored several others *who were also convinced of hallucinating into life after death* in the way of his preaching. He soon mentored many future holy homo-sapien leaders into proselytizing his ideas.

All these leaders in belief systems probably originated in the northwest of Africa, the Levant, and the Caucasus regions, but this is only a guess by the writer. The first holy-man could have originated anywhere for that matter, maybe in the Indian Chinese sub-continent regions. The origination of the bully-pulpit holy homo-sapiens could have been anywhere in the world, but the final domination of the ultimate new developments of faiths moved towards N W Africa. It is not much unlike: how USA, a young backward country *once upon a time,* dominates completely world power today. As an example, anyone from USA desirous of advanced studies as late as 150 years ago had to come over to Europe, because USA had no advanced educational institutions *then*! However, we do know from records of the last 10,000 years (i.e., the Evolutionary Modern Era) that the activities of the bully-pulpit holy homo-sapiens concentrated heavily in the regions mentioned near N E Africa. These early religious leaders may not have been initially "in cahoots" with the strong-armed, muscular big-bullies. The religious big-bullies dominated as leaders strictly through their mental abilities.

At some point, by the time of the appearance of these holy homo-sapiens, the muscular big-bullies had become powerful enough to take over roles as local kings or royalty in control of ever-increasing homo-whatever groups, but yet they deferred subjugating the religious big-bullies in the manner of commoners.

Thereby, all kings, big and small, are descendants of some strong-armed big-bully, surrounded by independent religious big-bullies.

A hierarchical system of a prime descendant of a king becoming the next king may have evolved just as homo-whatevers evolved into marriages, family, home bound life etc. *The newly crowned king* assured the guaranteed protection of the underprivileged in his group in return for their allegiance. The king's progeny always had the first and probably the only opportunity with advanced weaponry of their time and so hierarchy got well established naturally. In other words, the muscular big-bullies were gradually becoming local kings, controlling much larger groups after killing off neighboring rivals. This form of royalty and maintaining power through force could have also been initiated in the familiar northeast African regions mentioned, *but that is not certain.*

This may have begun 10,000 to 5,000 years ago before the beginning of The Evolutionary Modern Era. Regardless, it makes no difference where any new attitude of homo-*whatevers* got started, *if as long as the common attitude of prevalence was "kill them all",* every time one group faced another. Only the ultimate prevalent group and its location mattered for further conquests, and it happens to be "us".

This conjecture of crediting N E Africa for many epochal events is drawn from noticing an unusual concentration of religious-type leaders in these regions of northeast Africa (Nile River, lowlands), Levant, Caucasus, Anatolia, and present-day Iraq and Iran. Though often overlooked due to bias, the same level of recognition of progress should be given to the holy big-bully pulpits in the Asian regions of China and India. However, *in the near and far eastern regions*, the temperament of both the muscular big-bully kings and holy man big-bully pulpits were distinctly different than compared with other western regions of the earth. Here their brains opted to take predominantly the other tine in the options fork. This stark difference between the rise of belief systems between east and west has already been touched above.

The most important key point to understand here is that once groups with this new holy (religious) zeal began migrating to the far corners of the earth, *the furtherance and advancements religious ideas continuously evolving in northeast Africa did not have time to spread with the same intensity to far-off distant lands.* As homo-sapiens' conquests expanded, there came a time when they rarely went beyond 1,500 miles in any favored direction to spread newer ideas. This leads to another important point: The big-bullies, whether of the muscular kingly type or now the added the holy-man type, **spent large parts of their time building massive, self-glorifying ego-satisfying monuments** (Sphinx, Pyramids), rather than conquering new territories far off for conversion into their continuously advancing belief systems. In the location of all the large monuments and arts of long ago are testaments to this sort of egotistical behavior. *Not too many large monuments exist in far off Russian, Mongolian, Germanic, Celtic, and English lands, let alone Americas and down-under.*

Those in the far distant regions in relation to N E Africa were completely unaware of the new religious advancements or the towering artworks being created. That is why, in the far-off lands of Mongolia, Siberia, (even) the Germanic regions, the Americas, and the lands and islands of the down-under, we only see more primitive belief systems *accompanied by inferior art* before and during The Evolutionary Modern Era. These primitive systems may have been closer to how belief systems existed in the N E African regions *at the long ago start of belief systems.* Strangely, the earliest homo-sapiens (or those immediately before the homo- penultimates) who migrated to colder regions like far northwest Germanic regions of Europe and far north east Russia seemed to also lag in some key areas of vocal and language skills, musical and artistic advancements, advanced killing tools, *and the skills and desires of*

building large edifices. Of course, they sure caught up *with the advancements in science* and even surpassed the rest of the world much later on. The achievement in science belies the fact that they were backwards when faith-based systems were predominant elsewhere.

They also lagged in advanced supernatural concepts in relation to what was being practiced in N E Africa. You won't find many large structural artworks in these regions either. This proves that N W and W European regions also can be considered somewhat as far off lands in a way such as the Americas, for quite some time in relation to advancement of belief systems. But Europe was not physically as far as some of the other far-off regions and hence it caught up into the belief zeal with N E Africa quite fast (when compared to other far-off lands). Of the many drivers of homo-*whatever's* evolution, the continuing brain expansion was the chief character. The brain, for once, was uniquely expanding into regions of extra capacity as explained as region 3 – which is not necessarily a needed region, strictly speaking (illustration 13). This extra capacity, chiefly usable for thinking, feeling etc. (read: hallucinating and planning), pushed the brain to conceptualize (read: hallucinate) the ideas of supernatural, **god-etc.**

That is why, once the *false but charismatic ideas of **god-etc.***, took root, the creativity from that extra brain space of the homo-sapien spun out into many successful varieties of belief systems and further again into their offshoots. It merely started as one crude belief system from the first holy-man homo-sapien (illustration 9}. Each region catching up on the concepts of "to heaven after death" etc., adapted hallucinations in its own way, generating a spectrum of religions based on the same original fundamental impulses of *thoughts*.

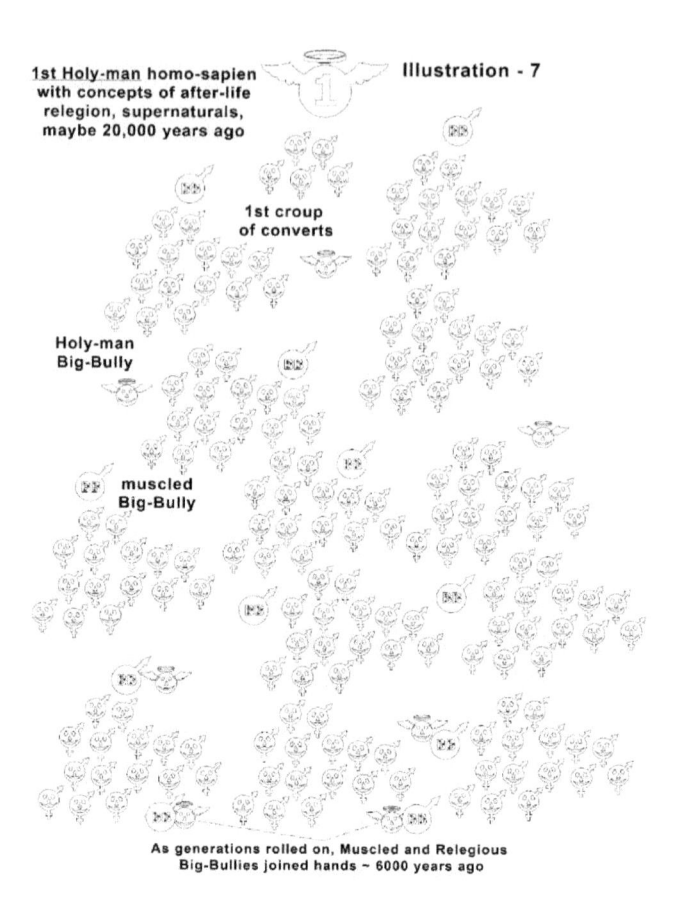

Illustration 7: This illustration shows the possible emergence of the *very first* charismatic holy-man homo-whatever with ideas of his brain's region 3 (thinking through hallucinations). He could have come on the scene among the homo-sapiens or the penultimates of them some 10,000 to 5,000 years before the beginnings of The Evolutionary Modern Era.

He likely is the first one who conceived (read: hallucinated) probably the idea of "life after death", the first one who convinced a vulnerable group of admiring homo-whatevers of the possibilities of the glory in the afterlife. Likely, he or some clever followers of his may have further introduced the ideas of heaven, hell, eternal *kingdoms* of gods, and some "cool" chanting rituals. (muscular big-bullies had upgraded selves into kings).

Did this happen about 5,000 to 10,000 years ago before The Evolutionary Modern Era? Maybe in the times when the homo-penultimates were still living, possibly among homo-neanderthalensis, when they were still around as neighbors with "us" homo-sapiens. Or maybe all of it was concocted by only "us" the homo-sapiens.

This first holy man must have sensed and *exploited* the growing fear of death among the normal members of a group. Weaving into daily living some rudimentary religion and rituals, probably including chanting and sacrifices, and possibly the first primitive concepts of the existence of a or some gods and spending one's afterlife with them in glory, he probably must have sold the idea that, after death, the family as a unit —male, female, offsprings—could stay together *forever* in some glorious *kingdom of gods, so long as they followed his teachings when they were alive.* Boy, that must have been music to the ears of the women-cum-wives constantly getting switched around into groups.

This writer can only imagine the zeal and excitement these new ideas must have caused within the lives of newly formed rudimentary families having rudimentary oral skills of communication.

Why was the holy-man able to craft these ideas? Simple. With full personal zeal, he unknowingly used his extra space region 3 within his growing brain to think and imagine (read, hallucinate). His hallucinations became doctrines for everyday living for homo-sapiens in proximity to him. That was the unfortunate path, *a wrong tine of the thinking fork* chosen by a holy-man who ultimately got self-attached to muscular big-bully to spread his influence *in force*. Imagine if that energy had been channeled into scientific investigation instead, which he could have! The potential was there all the time in the ready brain grown in size. But no, the newly developed homo-sapien's ego had already crept deep into the root of the paths of his thinking since eons, steering the homo-sapiens toward greed, hate, bigotry, power, and other destructive traits. None of such traits existed in his ancestral chimp bipeds.

Of all the evolutionary developments from chimps to homo-sapiens, ego and bigotry are the most dangerous and they are the deeply embedded inside negativity-ridden traits of the hominin species. And of those two, ego is the most damaging—because it's the hardest to recognize by self and eradicate. Even if recognized, ego is nearly untamable. In illustration 7, beneath the shown first holy homo-*whatever* are his few captivated and mentored followers. That was the beginnings of proselytizing. They go on to convert many others who become utterly convinced and surrender to a new way of life of worship and ritual that was set up according to their pandit-cum-guru. They become loyal to his new leadership and teachings. He has now become the (non-muscular) big-bully This moment marks the start of conversions, easily driven by the ideas from the expanding brain, which continued to grow.

The zealots weren't just converted; they were trained, mentored, shaped into the next holy homo-*whatevers,* and primed to spread their newfound beliefs to others. All this had nothing to do with reality or reasoning about nature in a humanistic way of looking for evidence.

This transformation into faith and belief systems likely began between 10,000 and 5,000 years ago before The Modern Evolutionary Era. The newly anointed believers ignited the fire of proselytizing in the migrants, spreading it like a contagion across lands. The writer believes that the zealotry of religiousness that spanned the last 2,500 years or so through several *ever-so-famous prophets* is child's play compared to what took place before The Modern Evolutionary Era. The mutual killing for its spreading must have been so widespread; *no wonder only homo-sapiens, us, the final and greatest killers remained.*

Illustration - 8

ALL of us homo-sapiens of last 10,000 years including,
You,
me, Copernicus, Newton, Einstein, Faraday, & the *Fab four*

Chimps & Bonobos

Various Homo-*whatever(s)*

Homo-Penultimate (Neanderthal?)

Homo - Sapiens
Homo - Luzones
Homo - Neanderthalensis
Homo - Denisovans
Homo - Naledi
Homo - Heidelbergensis
Homo - Erectus
Homo - Habilis
Austalopithicus - Aferensis
Ardipithecus Ramidus

Homo-Whatever C

Homo-Whatever B

Homo-Whatever A

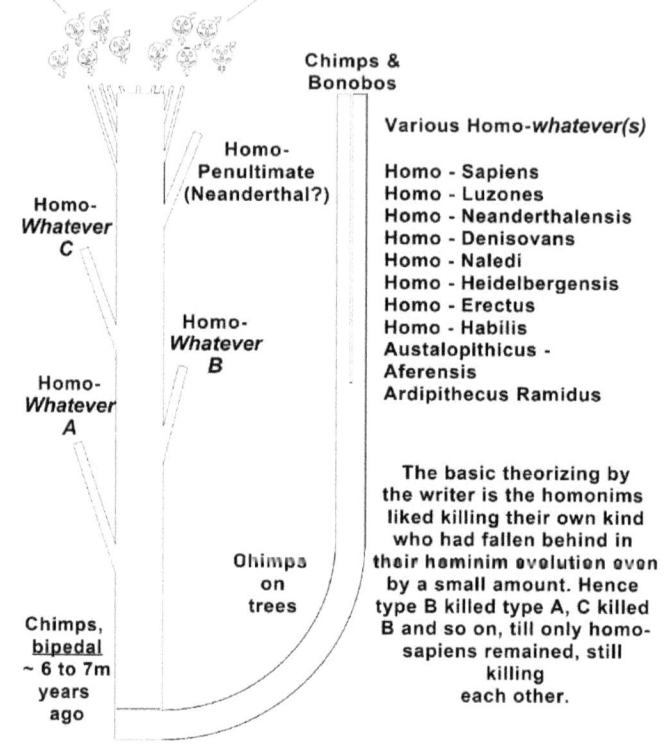

Chimps on trees

Chimps, bipedal ~ 6 to 7m years ago

The basic theorizing by the writer is the homonims liked killing their own kind who had fallen behind in their heminim evolution even by a small amount. Hence type B killed type A, C killed B and so on, till only homo-sapiens remained, still killing each other.

Illustration 8: This illustration shows a "tree trunk and its stump at base" — a style representing the chimps from over 6 million years ago shown at the trunk's base. The stump splits, marking a divide between tree-dwelling chimps and the earliest chimp bipeds. This divide was established around the time of 6 to 7 million years ago. The bipedal chimps as a new species must have appeared quickly and evolved and separated from the tree dwelling chimps, over several thousands of years as a new species. How long it took for some chimps to prefer and become full bipeds, and why they preferred so, is a question that will be answered, as this writer sees it. The new group is the emerging bipeds. They abandoned the trees and chose life on the ground. How did this shift happen? The writer has his own theory, which is explained through a different explanation soon to follow below. Don't necessarily buy into the other illustrations floating around that show a gradual lifting up of the torso in steps.

The original chimp group stayed in the trees, continuing as normal chimps. These chimps what we see today in Africa are the descendants of the chimps that remained as chimps in the trees. Some of these

later evolved into bonobos that are still chimp-like, and are still found in parts of the African continent.

Now, about those bipeds? They must have multiplied and evolved fast. Six million years from chimps to you and me is rapid in evolutionary terms, especially when you look at all the changes from a chimp to a homo-sapien. These bipeds became what the writer calls the remainder of the homo-sapiens of today, and they spread across the entire earth like no other creature ever did. This may be because they had so many reasons *and abilities to wander everywhere* in just 6 million years. The branched stumps on the trunk represent countless homo-*whatevers* (A.K.A. species) that no longer exist because inferior species was killed by the superiors.

At each branch the growing brain branched into a new variation of bipeds or homo-*whatevers* with enough variation to stand out as new species. The various scientific terms for the hominins given by researchers and experts are provided for reference in the same illustration. By and large, we do not care for these scientific names for our write-up, except maybe in terms of homo-neanderthalensis as being the penultimate homo-*whatever* to homo-sapiens = us.

As for the full disappearance of the older species, - what happened? How many do you think bipeds combined with hominins lived and died in the past 6 million years? 20 billion? As the bipeds and homo-*whatevers* died and lay on ground, their bodies probably lay discarded in the open to be devoured by scavengers. Taking care of a dead homo-*whatever* is a fairly modern method and must have not existed for most of the 6 million years. And so, their bodies must have been just left for the vultures and other scavengers. Bones and teeth do not generally get eaten and also do not get destroyed *easily*. Soooooo, there must be a lot more fossils out there to be discovered buried in rocks, unless they were pulverized to dust due to plate tectonics and volcanic heat. The writer contends the hominins did not vanish (read: go extinct) on their own. They were systematically killed by the more advanced homo-*whatevers* of their times at each step. This killing of one's own type into elimination is another feature the hominins developed for self. No other creature acts with such a singular purpose. The illustration lists the various names researchers have assigned to these long-gone hominin types.

Here is how the writer envisions the earliest conversion of a normal chimp to a biped happened: it surely must have been through a genetic mutation, probably accelerated by the established continued growth of the brain of a certain mother or father chimp. When a few chimp mothers, with their babes clinging to them, had gotten down from the trees, possibly near a water source, one of these chimp babies jumped off his mama and, instead of running on fours to another chimp toddler, he runs on his hind twos, simply based on his mutated genetics. His inherited genetics have made him to stay erect and bipedal, probably to the amazement of the adult chimps around him. His mother and father are the last couple in that lineage to be tree dwelling, but together they have created an offspring that prefers bipedalism and stay on ground. He was the very first to prefer the ground to play on rather than swing in the branches. He was our first daddy for new bipeds" evolution.

Additionally, after some investigations through the search engines, the writer found these:

Species	Timeframe	Location
Homo sapiens	~ 250 k / now	Us, all over
Homo-Luzones	~ 67 k years ago	Philippines??
Homo-Neanderthalensis	~ 400k to 40k	Europe
Homo-Denisovans	~ (400k to 50k)	China, Tibet
Homo Naledi	~ 0.3 my-ago	Gauteng, S Africa
Homo heidelbergensis	~ 0.4 my-ago	Europe, Africa and Asia
Homo Erectus	~ 2 / 0.15 m y-ago	Eurasia (Iberia to Java)
Homo Habilis	~ 2.1 my-ago	Tanzania
Australopithecus Afarensis	~ 3.5 my-ago	Ethiopia (Hadar)
Ardipithecus Ramidus	~ 4.4 my-ago	Ethiopia

THE KITH AND KIN OF HANUMAAN

Orrorin Tugenensis	~ 6 m y-ago	Kenya
Sahelanthropus tchadensis	~ 7 / 6 m y-ago	Chad, Africa

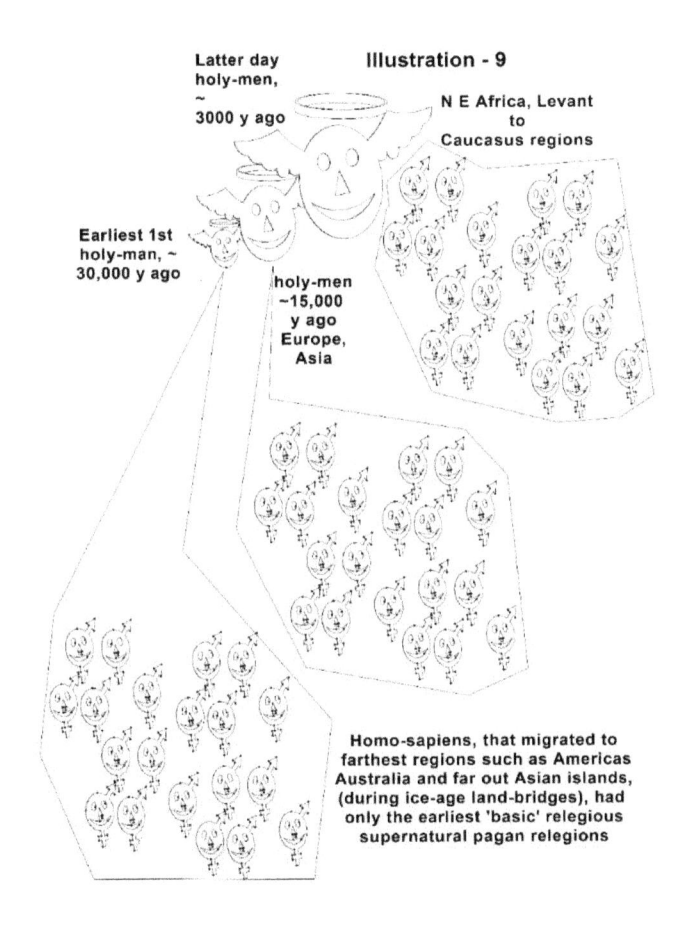

Illustration - 9

Latter day holy-men, ~ 3000 y ago

N E Africa, Levant to Caucasus regions

Earliest 1st holy-man, ~ 30,000 y ago

holy-men ~15,000 y ago Europe, Asia

Homo-sapiens, that migrated to farthest regions such as Americas Australia and far out Asian islands, (during ice-age land-bridges), had only the earliest 'basic' religious supernatural pagan relegions

Illustration 9: This illustration shows the evolution of a particular 1st holy-man homo-whatever, who probably emerged some 5,000 to 10,000 years ago before The Evolutionary Modern Era. The already sufficiently grown brain created this *real game-changer* in hominin living, the first ever "holy-man homo-sapien" who thought of (read: hallucinated about) life after death and gradually thought of other supernatural ideas, without realizing that they were all hallucinations which had full basis of his intellect *but had no basis in reality.*

His ideas must have been truly earth-shattering for the time when many homo-whatevers must have been establishing steady families, true family living, probably with *some form of "till death do us part" emotions* running around. Converts to this holy-man's ideas must have been fully captivated to his communicative skills (see enclosure on left). They became super inspired. You can see in the illustration a group of ordinary homo-whatevers who heard this 1st holy-man speak maybe vis-a-vis. The new converts and their descendants later migrated with zeal to distant lands. This group is indicated *on the left enclosure* of the illustration; it shows this original migrant group that had the temerity to wander off far right away. The wings and the halo are to indicate the holiness of the 1st ever preacher and respect given to him and the left enclosure indicates the earliest supernatural ideas imparted to *the earliest converts.*

This first holy homo-whatever, thus enlightened (read: hallucinated) in his own innocent way, is the one who laid the foundation for all the in-between religious (read hallucinated) troubles that followed for eons, and still continue today in lives of millions. His noble intentions, his love for fellow homo-*whatevers,* and his descendants that were led to concoct the earliest hallucinated ideas of **god-etc.**, and the concepts of rituals in daily life is indicated in the enclosure on left. The primitive rituals probably were not much different than similar to counting beads and chanting as done even today. Absolutely no relation to reality.

From that point on, chaos ensued as this writer can theorize, since none of the rituals or beliefs are grounded in reality with any evidence presented by the holy-man or his converts. ***They meant well***, particularly when it came to including many of the already existing morals, ethics, and possibly non-violence and groupism. All three concepts probably already existed before him and they don't need to be tied up with his **god-etc**. philosophy. Yet here we are, tangled up still in the many wrongful beliefs in supernaturalism of **god-etc**. *that need to be debunked in all religions* and live with evidence-based philosophies of humanism and science.

The depth of troubles (read= killings) that followed these zealots is almost incomprehensible. This first holy homo-*whatever,* possibly a homo-sapien, succeeded in mentoring a few followers—believers in his new brand of "wise, holy, big-bully-pulpit lecturing on religiousness." From what we can gather, these early religious figures were always male, and none of them realized their own egos that were preventing them from looking into the most important function of their brains—thinking of looking for evidence of what they were saying or being said to.

The "super-duper" influence of supernatural beliefs is undeniable, whether coming to them from up their leaders or going down from them to their converts. The earliest influenced holy homo-sapiens must have left a mark on every homo-*whatever* they encountered. Many of those new converts thus influenced, then wandered off with their own zeal, carrying the newfound beliefs to far-off lands, spreading those "untruthful and troublesome" ideas along the way.

Though they had the capacity to question the validity of their own thinking (read: hallucinating) *at any stage of zigzag backtracking*, their ego, and fears of questioning must have prevented them from any sort of rebellion against the new beliefs. Let this writer ask: Is there a "believer and faith type" reader of this write-up who has the courage to truly investigate the so-called beliefs he was instilled with, *as being the holy truths*, and present any evidence on those beliefs? Q.E.D!

These wandering zealots didn't have "physical" access to the many refinements (read = polishing and modifying the hallucinations) to the original belief system. Refinements to beliefs were constantly happening back at the primordial origin of the birth place of beliefs. Hence, these homo-whatever zealots who have now traveled to far-off lands, may be 2k to 10k miles away, and they maintained not the refined but the near original, crude, too-pagan, animalistic belief systems they carried with them well past the beginning of The Modern Evolutionary Era.

When investigating homo-sapien tribes in far-off regions, like down-under or the Americas, both being the farthest by distance, some of these original primitive belief systems hardly modified may still linger.

After several generational gaps of converts" training, the middle enclosed group of homo-sapiens in the illustration, being barely but still linked continuously to the primordial original holy-homo-sapien region did learn some new advancements of the religious ideas at the primordial region. Their teachings were preached and upgraded by the latter-day descendants who had evolved over hundreds or thousands of years from the original 1st holy-man preacher. These are now, today, the latter-day holy homo-sapiens, may be 1,000 years ago before The Modern Evolutionary Era.

The bully-pulpit males of our Modern Evolutionary Era weren't static. They also evolved. They also had the natural ego that they may not have been aware of. From crude leaders, they became more refined teachers, instructing followers on religion and religious procedures. The largest group in the illustration *on right enclosure*, were connected to the third holy bully-pulpit homo-sapiens on the right. They represent the modern-day "saints" as recognized even today, possibly those of ~1,000 to 2,600 years ago. These holy men of the recent past emerged after many generations of mentoring by holy men, closer to the latter third of The Evolutionary Modern Era.

Soooooo, what was the greatest shift proselytized by the "latest-day saints?" A clear disdain for polytheism (big deal! when any and every theism is hallucination anyway!). Why? What new hallucinations did they go through to preach this new wisdom? What instigated them to stick to "there is only one god, - **my god…..my god"!?**

The evolution into monotheism became the hallmark of these most recent preachers. **Scientifically speaking, zero-theism—i.e., no-theism—aligns fully with reality,** with no-theism being the better of the two words. In fact, the writer is embarrassed to even discuss this subject because *there never was such "a thing" one or any god or gods.* He does not feel embarrassed to do discuss the *falsity of* the idea that the sun went around the earth, because at least the sun and earth are real objects and it is quite difficult to detect for a common homo-sapien who revolves around who. No such reality exists in discussing god, gods, **god-etc**. Yet, it seems no one even considered the possibility of there is no such thing as god until about Darwin's time. The truth that there is "no god" is undisputedly proved based on scientific evidence. Before that, the concept of rejecting gods altogether wasn't on anyone's radar. Looking for evidence must have always been considered a show-off talk till the last 250 or so years.

Compared to the ego of any single individual, the ego of a group backed by a religious belief system is thousands of times larger and is very difficult to deal with, as Copernicus and Galileo found out.

(female) egg surface area = .00003 sq. in

.0002" (Fine thin human hair is about .002" thick compare!)

Single celled with half the genes

.005" Dia sphere

Single celled with half the genes

(male) sperm penetrating bullet area = .00000003 sq. in

Illustration - 10

Theoretically several thousands of sperms can crowd shoulder to shoulder to penetrate an egg

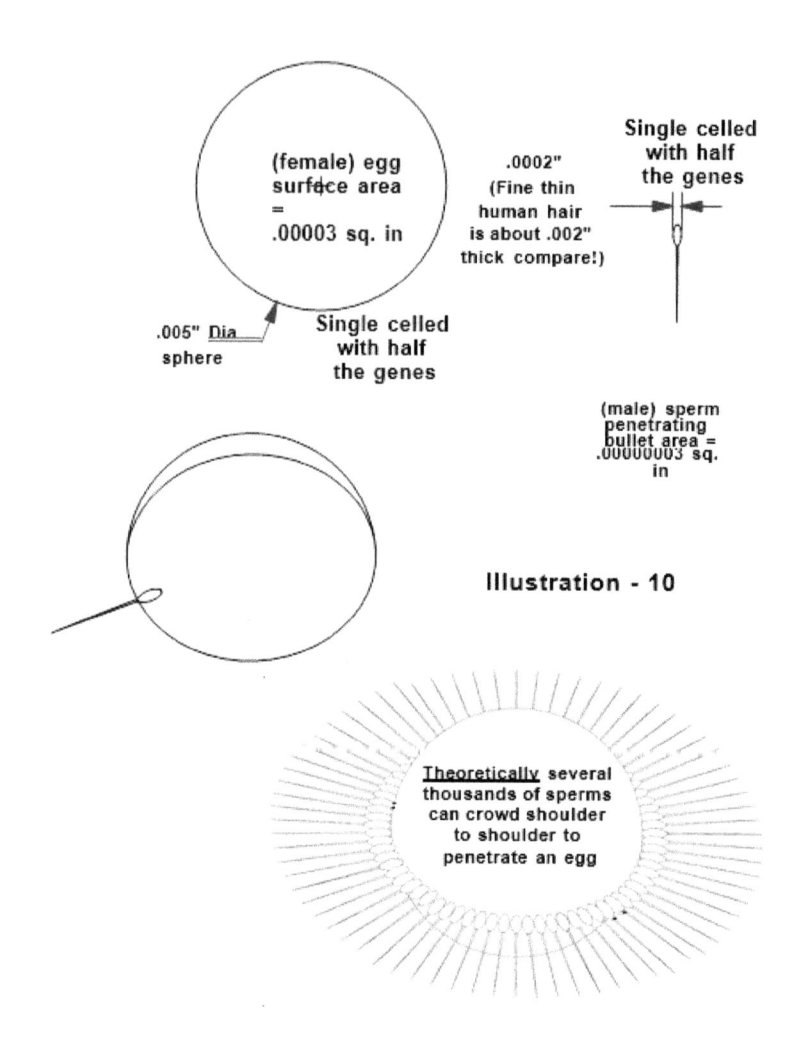

Illustration 10: Drawn to relative Scale: This illustration shows the depiction of a homo-sapien egg (a half homo-sapien? of course) and male sperm (the other half homo-sapien? again). The theoretical illustration, only for the sake of arguments, portrays multiple sperms attempting to penetrate the egg which should be a

theoretical possibility. So many millions of sperms, each single-celled *and individualistic half homo-sapiens* of future, **not visible to the naked eye**, none with fully identical "DNA" (read: characteristics) are released by a male uncontrollably with each ejaculation. All of them apparently know which way to go if they were expelled into a vaginal tract. Theoretically, it is possible and should be also easy for hundreds of them, shoulder to shoulder, to race toward the egg and penetrate it in photo-finish fashion. Why this doesn't happen often remains a mystery to this writer. Need some expert's input here.

It's said that only one sperm manages to enter the waiting egg, and even then, only its body—but not its tail, the writer was told. If true, this is a bizarre skillful act on the part of both halves to make a full (1/2+1/2=1) future homo-sapien. Something alive with a tail trying to penetrate its target but is allowed only partial entry. It is like you go for a movie with a ticket and the manager lets in only your head to peek through. A living force is restricted from using its full potential in the most crucial moment! Who controls this partial penetration, the sperm or the egg? Venture to say it is the egg, *because females always want to be always in control!* (hope you female readers see the humor, in this truth)

(even if the writer is wrong by 50% in his calculations below, the results are still staggering)

Here are some of the actual dimensions of the egg and sperm.

The diameter of an egg = 0.1 mm or 0.04 inches.

The diameter of a sperm = 3 micrometers or 0.00012 inches.

Hence, The surface area of the egg = πr^2 = 0.00125 in^2.

The penetrable area of a sperm = πr^2 = 0.000000011 in^2.

Soooooo, in theory – (0.00125 / 0.000000011 = ~113,600 sperms shoulder to shoulder arriving at the same instant at the egg's surface should be able to penetrate the egg!! **But only one does**! (Occasionally two). That is what the writer has been told. Some amazing numbers! Even if the writer is wrong in his calculations by a hundredfold, 1000 sperms in photo-finish should be doing **IT** in unison. Is this some weird form of friendly agreed-to raping?

Did you hear that when a sperm approached the egg eagerly for service, the egg asked, "What will you have, SIR?" The sperm replied, "I will have just one whole egg to go, *well done*" and the egg replied, "My

pleasure - SIR, you can have this one (showing herself fully naked), but you need to wait 9 months "of to-go-packaging" before it can be delivered for your take out."

Illustration - 11

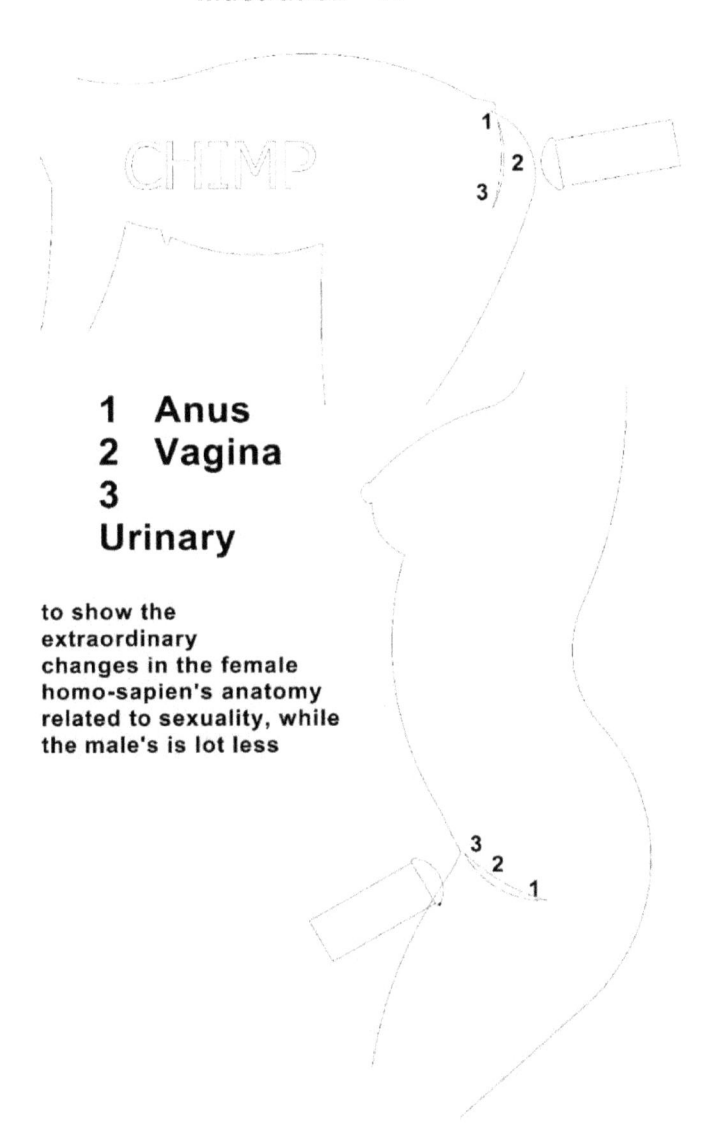

1 Anus
2 Vagina
3 Urinary

to show the extraordinary changes in the female homo-sapien's anatomy related to sexuality, while the male's is lot less

Illustration 11: This illustration shows the evolution and changes of a female homo-sapien's body in relation to sexuality, highlighting the angular variation in the vaginal canal between a female chimp 6 my ago and a modern homo-sapien female. The difference? Roughly 120 degrees of turn from rear to front for the **IT**-passage and also the other two. Only we hominins, homo-sapiens, are properly equipped to face each other while doing **IT**, though some bonobos also have evolved this frontal sex. Notice that with a bipedal couple in erect posture and having fully developed opposed thumbs, all sexually erotic parts of both the male and female are accessible to each other for extensive foreplay as desired. No other creature enjoys "soooooo much sex or foreplay".

It is difficult to theorize how and why the sexual nature of homo-sapiens has evolved to such a high degree of physicality when, on the other hand, other advanced creatures (mostly mammals) cannot even touch their own sexual organs either with their own limbs or can they be touched with the limbs of the other partner, except maybe in the case of primates that already have developed opposed thumbs. The opposed thumbs and flexible arms play an extremely superior role for homo-sapiens when compared to chimps. Chimps barely use their arms to hug each other during doing "**IT**", or probe each other's sex organs *even though they can* with their opposed thumbs. Small brains = less sex, it seems?

Illustration - 12

The female sexual anayomy must have gone through this orientation for a few hundred years before it settled to the present day orientstion

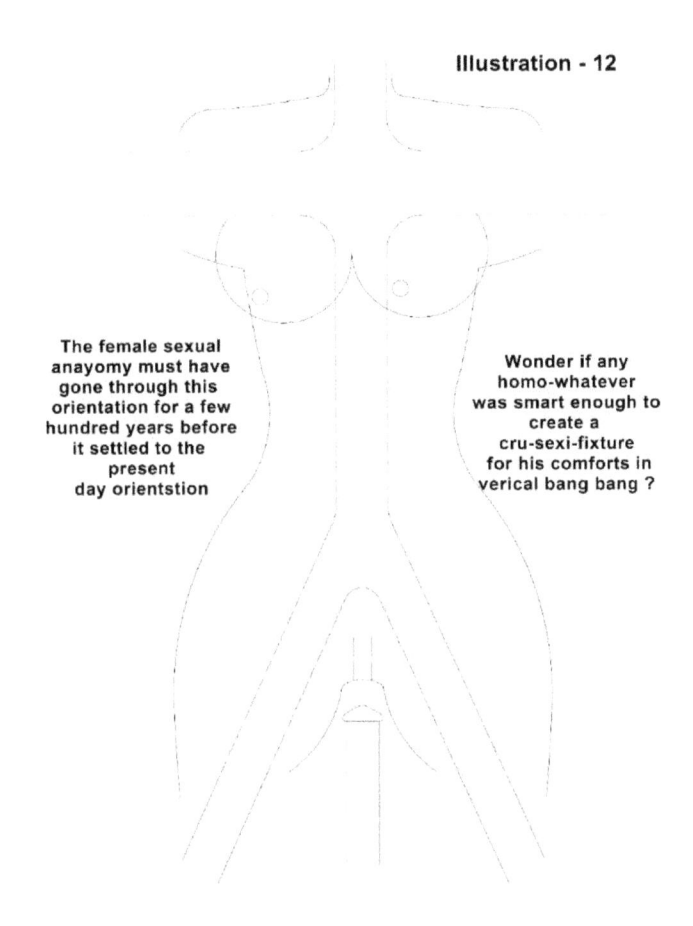

Wonder if any homo-whatever was smart enough to create a cru-sexi-fixture for his comforts in verical bang bang ?

Illustration 12: Similar to Illustration 11, this illustration shows another major variation that must have been as an interim, taken place gradually in the female anatomy's vaginal vertical tract. A female homo-sapien must have experienced slow angular rotation of its all three openings from the rear end of its body as in a chimp, namely: the anus, vagina, and urethra as a group. This must have happened as a single unit rotated over who knows how many hundreds of years.

For the male, it is a much easier task to adjust to the new angularity of the vaginal tract. But, - it must have been very amusing to witness if you could, though not impossible for male to do "**IT**", - when the female's vaginal tract rotated to plainly vertical. The writer theorizes that this position must have existed for hundreds of years before the vaginal tract rotated sufficiently forward to today's positioning.

Such a situation must have been heavily stressful for the mother while delivering a baby, requiring extra angular separation of the thighs. If this happened close to the beginning of The Modern Evolutionary Era, may be, we might dig up to find the fossil of a cru-sexi-fixture as shown, that made the male's job a bit easier and more pleasurable!

Illustration # 13

Ultra Simplified, Theorized 3 areas of the brain of a homo-sapien

Region 1: - the basic brain that handles all the bodily functions (similar to that of a chimpchimp)

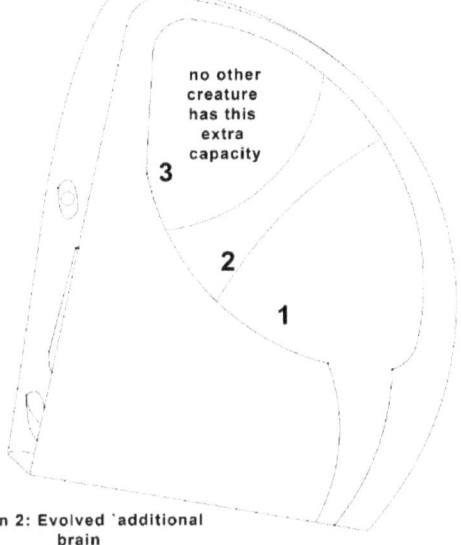

no other creature has this extra capacity

3

2

1

Region 2: Evolved 'additional brain for physical motions of vocals, hands legs, mouth, and lungs as related to vocals etc. (*Beyond* the capabilities of chimps)

Region 3: Evolved, extra space, for thinking (= hallucinating) emotions, feelings, interpreting, communicating non verbally & without any body motions, etc. (totally beyond chimp's capacity)

Illustration 13: This illustration is an *extremely* **super simplified presentation.** It is a theorized breakdown of the physical brain of a modern homo-sapien, measuring in at around 1,400 cubic centimeters. The brain is shown cut in half by a vertical plane of symmetry. Three distinct *hypothetical regions* are shown. These regions as shown have no bearing on the actual anatomy of a homo-sapien's brain. They are useful only to explain some theories for this write-up.

The first region; It reflects what a new bipedal chimp would have needed to function as a biped. This region represents everything a chimp's body needs to stay alive and function as a chimp. Think of it as a biped chimp's brain—nothing fancy, just the essentials.

The second region deals with advanced *bodily functions* in a hominin exclusive to homo-sapiens. This region is where all the real upgrades of the homo-sapien's skills are handled. Examples are advanced control over the super evolved voice box (say singing by the Fab-Four), precision at the opposed thumbs (say as needed by a surgeon for heart valve replacement), complex hand, torso and foot movements (say, Michael Jackson's Thriller's body movements), and some superior shoulder and hip joint movements. These advancements aren't found in chimps.

Now, the crown jewel—the third region. This is the ever-enlarging, generation to generation, "extra brain space." It is the seat of intelligence and higher thinking (read: hallucinating, planning, connecting emotions and memories). It is the seat for moods, feelings, memories, interpretations and so on. No other creature on the earth has anything like it. Region 3 is a luxurious space for deep thought, interpretation, symbolism, sexual fantasies, planning and dreaming, as well as planning *cheating*! This extra capacity is what sets homo-sapiens fully apart from everything else that knows to crawl, run, climb, fly, swim and jump around anywhere on this planet. *Most homo-sapiens are not aware how much extra capacity in brain they have by the time they reach adulthood.*

When someone says another person is only using a small portion of their brain, they're typically talking about this region not being exploited fully. Sometimes not even having the knowledge of its existence is the norm. This is where complex homo-sapien emotions, moods, symbolisms, memories, recalls, morals and ethics, bigotries, ego, love and hatred, and interpretations reside *and interact.* All that happens here are hallucinations at start, waiting for later to be used by the other two regions that control muscular movements as the outlets for thoughts.

What happens in region 3 has no direct effect on any muscle, until orders go out to regions 1 and 2! Plans for the future, moral or immoral ideas are hallucinated here. By and large, none of any activity happening in this region directly moves any nerve connected to any muscle until orders go to region 2 or 1 and muscular movement is activated. Put it a different way, when one is gently swinging in a hammock, eyes closed, ears and lips shut, palms under his occipital bone – but not asleep, it is this 3rd region of the brain that is active to the extent the individual understands the brain's use of this region.

The power of this region is undeniable. It has been used fully by *the holiest holy to cruelest homo-sapiens* that lived or are living. It can formulate to command a genius's mouth to deliver speeches that

influences millions. It can drive fingers with thumb to write words that live forever in homo-sapien created books (qitaabs). It can store here all the knowledge a surgeon needs to move his delicate tools with his exceptional fingers in the most precise manner.

About the growth and use of this region? First of all, it is necessary to recognize its existence by self or by being mentored about it. Its use depends on both:

1 recognizing its existence probably through mentoring individuals, and

2 the immediate surrounding external influencers that shape an individual's development right from infanthood. New emotions—ego, pride, greed, hatred, and bias—grow and circulate here. Just imagine a single neuron's cell based here may have 1000 dendrites connecting other neurons for information exchange that involves, - not yet, any muscular functionality. It houses the imaginative power (read = hallucination), which can create languages as powerful as mathematics, that can help create the most intricate real machinery or products, and also figure ways to understand the universe.

Anyone fully using this part of the brain holds the power to influence millions, for better or worse because common homo-sapiens are influenceable by sayings of charismatic individuals with their brain power. It can be used to investigate one's self or the universe's great truths. No other creature even comes close to possessing a miniscule portion of this region. However, mind you that nothing out there beyond the boundary of your skin, in the real world cares a hoot if you use this region 3 of your brain or not.

Section 6: Prompts Pointing to a Purpose

Basics: "Things" are either naturally made or creature made. The homo-sapien counts as to be unique but still is a creature. The real point here is "there is no such thing as god-made or god-created" anything.

Let the writer say upfront, the real purpose of this write-up is for homo-sapiens of the future, as individuals or as groups, for them *to stop killing other homo-sapiens* except for the occasionally needed *genuine reason* of self-defense. In other words, non-violence should be the rule of the day, any day, every day, always.

Over decades, there has been a steady conversion of this writer's inner self, the writer learning firmly that everything is either nature-made or creature-made, thus meaning made absolutely by no other. The homo-sapien is the greatest nature-made creature in almost every sense. He can build or destroy many things using what nature has given him: - the ever growing extra space in the brain (region 3, illustration 13).

He can manipulate others cleverly, who can manipulate even more of others with their own clever thinking, and so on and on through generations with no evidences needed of any reasons for doings or sayings. He can continue creating a belief system in all those homo-sapiens ignorant enough to be influenced, - that somewhere up there (the pointed direction is always up) is a great entity that creates all and makes rules for all. **Nothing is farther from truth**. Today, we know really very well all about all the stuff that is up there in any direction as far as one wants to see with naked eyes or super powerful telescopes of various types. There still are items like dark energy and dark matter, which we know exist but are not yet sure what they really are and we the scientists humbly accept our ignorance, for the 'now'. Is the faith minded ready to accept any ignorance?

With a system born out of hallucinations (= pure thinking) in region #3 of the brain as shown in illustration 13, many methods and, literally any possible methods and rules can be devised *just by thinking*. The hallucinator though being clever does not know that he is hallucinating. *Thinking is by far the weakest form to explain anything*, without being preceded by observation, and experimentation for establishing evidence.

By the way; there really is no permanent direction anywhere in this universe, such as up, down, front, back, left, right, east, west, north, and south except as perceived by the observer in relation to self. So, looking up with some manner of formed palms in gesture of obedience to some creator's attention is downright meaningless!

Looking at the illustrations, one must know and understand for a fact that *because of science* that the universe is aged to be about 14 billion years old. This has been proven over and over, literally by 1000s of researchers. With the availability of nature's numerous complex physical and chemical elements and inexhaustible time of billions of years, and inexhaustible energy for physical and chemical processes, nature has created numerous complex biological processes by using just a few naturally available items. This in turn created numerous creatures and plants that can duplicate themselves. Given such a long time to come up with anything, and with so many resources of materials and natural processes made readily available in the presence of various forms of energy, - *with abundance of time*, in the ever-mutating environment of an ideal "body" called earth, it is not such a big surprise anymore that we homo-sapiens evolved. And -by George- we have got what it takes to keep unraveling nature's acts.

That we descended from primates and not another creature seems to have had such a chance luck of the primates. We could easily have descended from felines, canines, horses, or some other creature. Lots and lots of interesting changes have evolved in the mere last 6 million years or so in the making of us, homo-sapiens, **while we must have eliminated all other hominins, by killing them.**

The changes in our evolution are so interesting that this writer could not give up tackling and theorizing the possible scenarios in the gap of 6m years. In such a short period the manner in which "these changes had taken place in the real" is astonishing when compared with other evolutionary changes. Just picture a female chimp's descendants of 6m years ago transforming their descendants to arrive at Marylin Monroe of just a few decades ago! Picture the chimp and her side by side.

You are also welcome to do the theorizing unless you believe too strongly in the supernatural creator and reject all science. Rejecting science and math means possibly no job for you; believing in a creator is not assurance of a job.

This writer has slowly changed – forever – not by just doing new things—not just through advanced education—but by taking a deep curiosity in "the *remainder* of 56.5 million square miles of the land mass of the earth", when compared to the 1.3 million square miles of the country he was legally confined to while growing up, in the contiguous first 21 years of his life in a fully colonized eastern country.

Today, most of us are not confined anywhere and can run around freely almost anywhere on this earth, inclusive of oceans and the air. An individual when young, is confined to an area probably less than 15 x 15 ft. square, his room, for most of his formative life. When the individual matures fully, say, aged 25 years and beyond, after all his schooling is done for, he starts covering larger grounds through employment or other. But by then "things in his far-flung wide personality" have already been strongly-wrongly influenced and solidified silently over the years of growing up, even though physically he hung around within the minuscule confines of his room.

Our personality traits reflect us and even if we give others the impression that we have visited far-off lands or stayed put in one place. The earth as a whole is *visited by many of us mentally*, only, aided by the constant camaraderie of instant telecommunications with many other homo-sapiens living in far-off places, or by us being glued to the plethora of multiple media outlets such as electronic pads, phones, computers, and TV. Only occasionally do we read hard-copy newspapers, magazines and books for knowledge and news. *Rarely we question the validity of what has been communicated to us through media* and **that is a real problem**. Go figure, two people with 3 medias can create 6 communications, 3 with 3 can create 18 communications, and there starts the unbelievable exponential growth. Which communications will you trust? how many communications have you forwarded today?

Who do you know that actually read War and Peace *fully?* The writer hasn't.

Even if we never go far from home, we still form solid, albeit biased, opinions of far-off places and of those who live *over there*. Even if an old homo-sapien has lived actively for 75 years anywhere far and wide, he still will have very few firsthand experiences about the world at large, but he can impress others as if he knows everything. These pseudo-experiences become not fleeting parts of our lives but a large part of our instantly referable *everyday biases, occasionally leading up to full bigotry*.

Such pseudo-experiences that are not visceral—say, like one's real play on a soccer field or tennis court, or like the required vis-a-vis trips made to college lecture rooms and grouped with others, or like the visits to a variety of frequented places such as restaurants and amusement centers— cannot be permanently internalized. Take-outs do not count as restaurant visits. In fact, the exponential rise in take-outs reveals the weakness of the homo-sapien, his drastic reductions in - the desire to brush, bathe, change, dress-up regularly, sit in proximity to others at eating establishments without staring, - take the chance with the entire family being ready to sit together, and by all means shut off all mobiles so as to converse. Even a young loving couple has trouble conversing romantically at an eat out session, for they have to look away from the phone. Forced to be by self? – then the gym is the perfect recluse to catch up with texting; 5 pushups followed by 5 minutes at the mobile screen. Uyyay-yayyay-yay....

Fake experiences can be forgotten as and when we choose. Still, in many pseudo mannerisms, we are constantly developing more and more needless biases rather than true knowledge about the real world. This is a complicated evolving subject for any homo-sapien to live with, and all big-bullies take advantage of this weakness.

Many pseudo-experiences of our tender years, forcibly impressed upon us by *benevolent yet ignorant caretakers*, have made a deep impression on us to be the real experiences, and *we grow to love living with them*. Ever wonder why they are forced upon us in the first ~ 6 years of our lives with full dominance by parents?

The early-on instilled biases since infancy remain with us even when we move out to live elsewhere, and again to another elsewhere, as "temporarily permanent" people. Our formed opinions and biases *generally* turn out to be useless and wrong. As for the writer, he has never been a native of anywhere any place, no matter where he lived for over 8 decades and had to make real efforts to be rid of early-on instilled home-based-biases for self and in others who dealt with him regularly.

No matter how much he tries, he never seems to blend in to be considered a native anywhere by the native-natives, as though it is their privilege to judge the writer as an anti! — and now that is the real bigotry of the native-natives! Name the region where you grew up and which you left a good 50 years ago to live elsewhere; the native-natives will still push you back to-there, i.e., to-where you grew up, ***ad nauseam*** *in conversations.* We never really fit in anywhere after we make our first move past about age 25 to far off places. So, even if we live in our fully adopted place in a sort of a foreign land, we are constantly adjusting to fit in it, and struggle with others to let it be our own place too.

One day, this writer read something that really hit hard into realization. His eyes bulged out of their sockets, and his mouth gasped open when he was made to understand the meaning of what came across in a few lines, as explained below in the background of the write-up. *There is a benefit as well as misery in staying curious* about the past, present, or future.

The background of this write-up has two distinct parts:

One - That no matter where each one of us is at this very instant, on land, in or on water, or in the air, everything surrounding us and whatever is under us has its own 4+ billion years of history. No two ways about that no matter where you are on this earth. That is the latest greatest history of this earth revolving since 4+ billion years.

Two - You, this writer, and the rest of all things presently living are breathing, eating, drinking, and excreting the same elements, atoms or molecules of water, air, oxygen, carbon, nitrogen, sulfur, phosphorus, etc. that others breathed, ate, drank and excreted. All of the 92+ or so elements on the earth, and many compounds, originally came from distant stars that exploded millions to billions of years ago and circulated through gazillions of creatures on earth before you and this writer ingested-digested the same. In that respect the earth has been the same whether it is for you today or for your ancestors several hundred years ago.

Our earth cannot make any elements of any kind. We all rehash the same old stuff over and over again that came originally from stars. Rarely any process on earth **pulls out an atom** from a more complex molecule, like photosynthesis.

You see, the biological processes are better at creating complex things like RNA, DNA, etc. but not making simpler things. This bears well with "thinking" which creates complex faith systems and their books, than simply looking for evidences and say voila!

The most serious permanent conversion that has taken place in the psyche of the writer is that he completely trusts in the continuation of natural evolutions in the universe. He trusts that all that is in *those natural processes* for the living or non-living to be true. and that there has never been a supernatural creator controlling these processes. He depends on fellow homo-sapiens to behave maturely and responsibly in the common involvement of attending to the resources of this planet for thousands of years to come. **No one is going anywhere, leaving this earth in any direction to colonize!! Don't you believe any big-bully of any type telling you otherwise.**

This earth is all we have for eons in the future.

The writer does not believe in anything even remotely similar to **god-etc.,** because there never was such

a thing or person and can't even fathom how that word ever got invented. Everything is either nature-made or creature-made, especially by advanced creatures like us, and less advanced like the birds, the bees, and the ants. There never was such a thing as a creator until we hallucinated him from thin air using our brains and successfully spread the primordial falsity.

The writer does hallucinate in a new, wonderful, modified culture with artforms for the future, based largely on science and devoid of supernatural superstition, evolving fully into new ways of scientific thinking culture.

The process will have the pains of deviating from the existing arts, music, drama, and culture *that have been developed for so long*, based maybe innocently but on false beliefs. He trusts in developing new art forms that are true to the universe as they really should be.

The two freedoms our large brain has given us over other creatures is that we have the enormous extra brain capacity (region 3) to think (read: hallucinate) anything. We constantly think to say what we want to say, but often say something else not matching our original thinking but in tune to some altered thinking. No one can detect or know about the homo- sapien's correlation between his thinking to say and utterings something different on the same related subject. Said in a different way: Animals do not have *luxury of lying.*

Section 7: When Did We Begin? Are We There Yet? Where Are We Going?

Do you know of *ANY* religious teaching, any book, qitaab, testament, 'holy-book' that starts with these paraphrase-able sentences:

"The WHOLE PURPOSE of living is to live it fully, with cheer, health, enjoyment, intense curiosity, happiness and camaraderie with all. With all that is available right here on earth presented to you, explore! **With a caveat for morals, ethics, and non-violence,** your living should be a glorious experience till the end of your life."

Why no book of life's guidance begins with something straightforward and simple like that? Most books expect you to sin and then define sin? How did all these religious books create all the useless text in them?

Your death, of course, is certain, but its manner may not be. Any alleviation of the realistic pain of impending death is alleviated through well-directed science of today's medicine and surgery, but never through the quackery of faith, hope, and prayer. Further, anyone else who proclaims "I will be back" and goes away through death, **he is never coming back,** and good scientists and the writer know it. A duped religious person wastes time on counting beads and hoping for miracles. Sadly, this kind of ignorance is most plentiful in the really poor and ignorant people of this planet, because they are so easy to convert and it is so difficult to revert to sanity. All those who were born and lived **before** knowing anything about evolutionary science, microscopes and telescopes, - all those that lived faith based, that believed in all that is creative thinking and hallucinations, - no matter how much knowledge and great qualities they had, **they knew zilch**.

We now know quite a bit today, maybe not all, but enough about the universe. We know how and when the universe was born, and how it progressed to this date, to this state, including our solar system. That quest of learning never stops.

Yes, our brains are now naturally big enough for us to have dominion over all living things, not because some non-existent god gave us the power though quotes in "books, qitaabs, testaments, commandments, scrolls", but because of the quirk of genetic mutation in some chimp that inherited brain growth let us become cleverer beyond belief.

Misuse of this brain power at this stage will only cause mutual destruction of us and as much to the earth. In hopes with our deep curiosity in looking for aliens, if we do find any, **we may find their fossils only!;** which would prove that they "mutually foolishly destroyed themselves" long time ago *in a fashion we are likely to follow.*

Hope, faith, prayers, and such **god-etc**. hopes *are selfish, egotistical, in vain, and downright quackery;* whereas evidence seeking observations, examinations, reasonings, are true processes for all to live by. All-encompassing compassion and universal benefits are to be the byproducts.

Nothing sparks your intelligence like genuine curiosity to know all that is possible to know, - to know about anything and everything in the universe. *Why not study "your inner fish" as described by Neil Shubin and get inspired.* Fortunate is the one who is very curious about real nature as it must have truly evolved!

We need to constantly study, learn, and correct ourselves through compassion, morals, ethics, reasoning, and reasonable attitudes toward pacification, - and we should really care to use self's region 3 to the fullest. Someone is always be ahead and more powerful and cocky. But misuse of that will be a big mistake that might pulverize our own fossils.

Now, evolution is a very, *very*, **very** slow process. Can you force yourself to walk from your bed to the bathroom at a steady pace in not less than 24 hours? Evolution is probably much slower than your walk, and it is unrelenting. The process of coming from a regular chimp to a bipedal chimp and then finally to a homo-sapien has been slow. Time taken for Chimp to become a biped may be unknown, but from bipeds to us homo-sapiens is estimated at about 6 million years. This slowness of homo-sapien evolution is not as slow as when compared to the first *tough-finned fish* that first decided to walk out of water on to the beaches and acquired amphibian living for better security for self and its eggs. There was no one living on the beaches or beyond then! Its descendants gradually evolved into four-legged reptiles first, and then into mammals, just like today's wolves or deer, among others. Hundreds of millions of years elapsed before the fish **Tektaalik** turned into dinosaurs and then into mammals inclusive of primates / chimps.

What does all this slow process mean? When and how did the first life start? That is the toughest question, but one answer for sure is, there definitely was no *creator who made such things happen*. Stanley Miller and Harold Urey already created a primordial soup very similar to those living things of today are made of, about 75 years ago in their lab. It resembles, in its raw form, what living things are made-up of. That is just one step in the making of living things to become alive.

It is possible that life was generated into a bio-mass during the natural evolutionary process, starting with some such primordial soup that got subjected to all the mutations, energies, and forces available in nature **over a few billions of years** in very tiny random mutating steps with no conceived goal to make the living that which the thing turned out to be, and now it can duplicate itself. Much before the bacteria/virus got created, much simpler living things must have been generated *naturally*. With constant experimentation, this process will be figured out in our labs someday. That will be the day the never existent creator will vanish from all minds.

None of us can perform continued experiments even for a few hundred years with constant interpretations of results and adjustments, while nature has billions of years at its disposal with huge amounts of materials and energies to experiment with myriads of ways. *If in a given space,* both materials and energies are present in their fundamental form, then some sort evolutionary process *will go on continuously*, turning out new products. In fact, after the very first life evolved in water, about 3.5 billion years agio, it stayed just about the same as the original microscopic life for close to 3 billion years mutating very slowly, because in the confines of the oceans, material and energies were always present.

Hopefully, in the next 100 years, enough experimentation can be done to prove without a doubt the possibility that *cellular life can start on its own* from a primordial soup after it is subjected to more and appropriate experimentations. Darwin, primarily with some others, proved through what is termed natural selection that every living creature, through a mother father pairing, is made to be an *almost* but not exact duplicate candidate of their combo. It always deviated a teeny bit from their pure combination. Within many kids of animals growing up in a group, only the "fittest toughest" get the opportunity to do **IT** and create new offsprings. This "natural selection" is the key euphemism for what turns out to be that only the muscular big-bully type hominin produces babies through many females under him. **Nature is unfairly mean**.

The new baby is never exactly the same as the mother or father or even halfway either because mutations always occur when cells start duplicating after conception. With enough mutations and time, we have then a new creature that barely resembles its ancestors and is a now a new species and can no longer do **IT** with the old types.

Our ancestors would not admit their ignorance often enough. Lack of available tools and methods failed them in proving many of the natural phenomena that we can prove almost instantly today. In short, they *simply thought and said things they thought* would be the right answers. They *simply thought,* very intelligently, of course, and said anything that they themselves were convinced of, without ever looking for evidence. **Nature doesn't give a damn to anyone's intellect or knowledge or thinking.** *But it can not hide from their observations and experiments.*

But in today's research, every legitimate (read - non-egotistical) researcher's report starts with the following *unwritten, unspoken words*: "this write-up could be erroneous in finding these stated results that are being published, but here is what I have found after numerous observations and experiments that I performed myself or supervised as listed, with evidences and reasonings attached. Feel free to check me up thoroughly and look for any chinks in the armor." No researcher of today can escape prompt fact-checking of his findings by others.

In consideration to the unlimited time nature has to evolve strange life forms, look at the 17-year cicada, starting as a tiny egg buried inches into the soil, with no visible clock ticking in it. It knows *when to wake up after 17 years*, climb up a tree, and change its outfit before doing its only goal—its itching duty— the itch that makes it scream all day long with its wings flapping, and then doing **IT** with a female counterpart. Once that part is over it decides to simply die. The lady Cicada hangs around a bit longer, does her part producing eggs and dies too. The eggs get buried in the soil at the roots of the trees and do not show up exactly for 17 years!

Amazing? This may also explain why males die earlier than females *as a general rule*: once the male does **IT** with the female, his job is done; he goes to sleep soon enough, often probably with no intention of waking up. However, the female has to carry the eggs from birth to maturity and so lives longer. Voila ladies, that is why living longer is a built-in, in you! When a group of a few mother chimps carefully ventured to the ground and walked on all fours to a nearby pond for water while their babies were hanging on piggyback using all four opposed digits. The babies as yet would not let go of their mothers—all except maybe one kid. He was a different chimp who would frequently jump off mama and run on twos to the other "clinging-on kids" to play with. This kid probably already had a mutation in his DNA at birth that made him prefer to be on his hind twos, right from the start. He may have been a novelty among other chimps who preferred to run on four limbs all the time when all were playing on the ground. He at maturity, produced a few boy and girl kids who also carried on like the new biped, preferring to be bipedal and on the ground, as soon as they could let go of mama.

Don't you agree with this theorized explanation? If not then, let's see what explanation you can come up with.

What we require is to be passionate about in guessing what could have factually happened in the past, with as much correct detail as possible, even if it was a long time ago. Accurate history started only a few hundred years ago but *all of the past going back eons did happen*, as evidenced by the present and some written and oral records. *We are itching to know the real facts;* let us ask Kipling's friends: how, why, when, what, who, where. Let us micro-investigate, theorize, argue, etc., how "**us**" started on two legs, moved about, screwed around doing **IT** a lot more than any creature could dream of, and how we behaved through the last 6m years + 10k. We both may be unique, but really, we both have been only uniquely recycled through a "very long-distance incestual relationship". Mating between close cousins may be considered incest and harmful, but all homo-sapiens that interact sexually are cousins *way back from the past,* with no harm incurred. There is some form of far distant incest always involved. ***No one is created brand new not related to some existing creature.***

Bipedalism definitely must have been due to a gene mutation whose reason is from the perennial brain growth. Bipedal chimps must have preferred bipedalism to tree-dwelling to the annoyance of other tree dwelling chimps. The writer feels bipedalism was by and large almost an instantaneous change!

Several times, as the earth cooled for hundreds to thousands of years and snow accumulated in many land areas, especially in the polar regions, the ocean levels were drastically lowered, exposing several shallow sea bottoms to become land bridges. These land bridges facilitated all creatures living on large continents to cross across and occupy the temporary low drylands to simply live there. All sorts of animals and homo-whatevers must have used these low-lying areas either to live semi-permanently on these land bridges or travel as and when they needed between the larger continents, of which they knew nothing. Of course, none of them knew what they were doing except knowing that there is land under their feet. There should be many interesting fossils of homo-*whatevers* buried in these low-lying land bridge areas that are covered by oceans today! It is possible that these large land areas created islands before being fully drowned as snows melted. That process could have trapped homo-sapiens and other creatures on the temporary islands with no escape and to eventual death by drowning. Think we can excavate such fossils?

We have so much extra brain capacity that we have become accustomed to consult permanently all the six friends of Sir Rudyard Kipling every time—how, why, when, what, who, and where which is the coolest way to do research. Call all of them together as "the curiosity group"- our greatest friend. However very few homo-sapiens use the curiosity group *in depth* to advance their knowledge.

The ancients were very smart, but nowhere does this writer come across utterance by them with words like "we don't know because…" They had no inkling looking into evidence-based data, tinkering to be knowledgeable about the reality of anything. **They were simply great at thinking and that is neither enough nor correct.**

We both may be unique, but really, we both have a beginning through uniquely recycled "very very long-distanced incestual relationship"

Section 8: A Half's Half-Poke into the Second Half

These little wiggling ball players (AKA male sperms) were running frantically for the humongous ball (AKA female egg). The winning sperm represents only half a homo-sapien, and the egg in waiting represents also just a different half homo-sapien. All the homo-sapiens who walked this earth did not know anything about this half-and-half sperm-egg process until about 450 years ago till the microscope got perfected.

All those who believed in the supernatural, miracles, and any myths about newborns were wrong! Some even believed in birth of a whole homo-sapien without the meeting between the two halves, which, of course, is impossible. A sperm poking into an egg may be very special for homo-sapiens, but the same process happens millions upon millions of times in all mammals each day! The birthing process is very complex for all advanced creatures, but no ordinary creature mama gets the care and attention of a homo-sapien mama.

Though those ancient homo-sapiens were deluded, a lot of credit is still due to all the well-known ancient greats (you know who it is for you!), because we are the recipients and followers of their excellent art, music, languages, ethics, morals, etc. Their faith of course is based on false beliefs of supernaturalism. A very often repeated incident occurs when all the little tail-wiggling half players want to play ball, but the ball is not there. It seems the egg presents itself only a few days each month for play ball and then it dumps itself out of the body in not necessarily a simple way. Too bad, enjoy the play, but no ball or goal this time. Only homo-sapiens do **IT** with a ball or no ball.

Until the magnifying glass and its complex versions of microscopes with multiple lenses were well developed, no one in the world must have known about the tailed swimmers called sperms. Besides, they swim in droves by hundreds of millions with each full "episode of uncontrolled squirting", which cannot be stopped once it starts. They were destined to swim for the very first time with a goal to reach and a ball to meet, a steady, unmoving ball—one egg in waiting—about which they must have known nothing. Did each one of these half players know *his only goal individually?*

Can you picture this alternate scene: the entire 100+ million homo-sapiens of a region running around looking for that one thing that they would know only when one of them bumped into it? An equivalence: If you live in a country with hundreds of millions of homo-sapiens, just as each homo-sapien is unique, these wigglers are also uniquely half-individuals, different from each other. Each one could have demanded a unique passport if he became whole. If conception occurs with each one of them, with the same half egg (one at a time of course), a different unique homo-sapien would be born each time! All those greats of the past whom we revere so much for their knowledge, and all those who listened to them and believed in their teachings about miraculous births and conceptions, must have known zilch as far as these *microscopic details* are concerned in relation to birth. Conception and birth are very natural common processes, even if extremely complex. After the rendezvous between sperm and an egg, recipe of making a baby starts cooking in a clockwork fashion, non-stop. These situations are not miracles, except that amazingly only one sperm out of the 100 million or so is generally *allowed in* by the egg. Each day billions of creatures are born, and the process is same or very similar. *It is just that we pay unique attention to homo-sapien births.*

The picture is of a new homo-sapien coming into this world for the next 100 years. It is not an easy mental task for all involved. It puts tremendous pressure on the thinking capacities of *many brains*. For animals there is no such pressure about the future.

No wonder, during ancient times, the birth of a baby was often referred to as a miracle. ***It is nothing of that sort***. In that respect, a gazillion things in the universe and life on earth could use the same term miracle. Such a superbly natural process of birth has been happening trillions and trillions and trillions of times for billions of years, once the knowledge of the processes of life's duplication by cell division through DNA duplication was established. One may say these are constant repetitive miracles for two lucky halves or looking at it a different *way it is large-scale destruction of just about 99.9999% of wannabe halves.*

When 100 million+ wiggling sperm tails dart to meet up with just one lady date, even if 99.5% go in the wrong direction or at slowed speed, we still have half a million rushing in the right direction. Can you picture 10 college football stadiums emptying, giving a running start to all the spectators, and then all the fans gravitating towards the quarterback to hug him? The sperm charge inside the female's vaginal tract must be much more chaotic than that.

The writer has heard the phrase "low sperm count" (refer to illustration 10). *Nonsense!* He cannot possibly believe in such a thing. All it takes is a dozen of the wigglers to go in the right direction for the "egg hunt". Maybe let us explain low sperm count as, - all the sperms being mutated at their birth to take wrong turns or swim sideways only—or maybe, because a certain male's penis-passage happens to have a sharp U-turn for reabsorbing the sperms into the testicles. They just want to go back into his testicles. Or, the egotistical sperms (males) must all be imbued with the most common attitude of male pride: *not asking for directions*! Low sperm count just to meet up with one measly female egg-in-waiting makes no sense. Opposed to low sperm count, no sperm count, as when a male's tubes are tied, makes a lot more sense. Each one of the 100+ million sperms is literally a unique guy; in other words, each is a unique half-male homo-sapien who just hasn't lost his tail yet, being ever ready to wag it for his half-lady date.

How is it that a male homo sapiens body is able to produce so many unique sperms so frequently? Every time the guy jerks off due to uncontrollable desires, every few hours during peak production periods of his youth, he literally is wasting away probably billions of would-be-dudes? That is at least half a billion unique and futile half-guys, each hitting the dust day in and day out for years!

What secrets can two or more small lenses placed in front of each other reveal secrets in relation to doing **IT**? You can look at a sperm with a microscope; it is too small for the naked eye. Compare-you can look at the details of Jupiter's moons with a telescope; they are too far for the naked eye.

A male homo sapiens" squirt contains about 100+ sperms, and he can have wasteful wet dreams. Many other mammals squirt out 500+ sperms. They don't waste any through wet dreams. How about two sperms vying for a photo finish for the win? Rarely does more than one winning sperm get the opportunity to crack the egg's shell; -that is what we hear. The female has thousands more eggs stored elsewhere for future plays. But the future for the winning sperm is now. *Does this half-guy know at least half of what he is getting into? Does he realize also what he is making all others in the world get into?*

The writer has been told that the wall of the egg closes shut the instant the winning sperm's body only penetrates the egg's wall! How in the heck does the egg know its boundary has been breached? Further, how can it react so fast? On his epic journey, has a sperm not encountered other obstacles in the vaginal tract and penetrated by mistake the vaginal tract's wall? The wiggler has no eyes, no nervous system, or arms with opposed thumbs of his own to stop other intruders from interfering with his goal!

Does the egg get a chance to look around at all the rushing Romeos closing in on her and yells, "Not you, you there, stop! Not you either, stop right there; I want that guy in the corner to dance and poke with"? Does such selective rejection happen?

If the egg and sperm become a "wholesome" *female,* after coming out into the world and maturing, it probably recalls how to play the rejection game. It is now a lady and employs all the womanly tactics. If the wholesomeness happens to be a male, he likewise, after coming out and matured, displays all the insecurities he faced in that "long and winding vaginal road" into a winning swim. When out and is become a homo-sapien, he runs around chasing the damsel of his choice, fighting all others in the way. There you have it! The politics between male and female that were already a part of them when they were still halves and not yet met! Can you picture this: the egg surrounds itself with fairly penetrable walls because it has to be so, ready by the rules to invite just one guest? She does not know which way he will enter her spherical finish line. The instant the winning Romeo comes through its wall, it instantly reconstructs the walls to make it impenetrable, like a fortress that no one else can break through, so it seems? Do you think the female half is looking for the most handsome sperm-half?

Really? Can't believe this half-baked story between the two halves getting together as halves, while millions of others become the half-have-me-nots. Sounds incredible. Just explaining away the above scene of a half meeting a half may be cute and just too darn easy. But languages are so useless to explain this complex, strange but common phenomena of sperm meeting egg and then all that happens thereafter – even if you are fluent and use twenty languages for your explanations, you will fall short. Let us go on a bit more before giving up. After success upstream by the one half-guy, do all the slower sperms get to know that they have lost the race, say by because they were hopelessly slow? Do they wander around the vaginal racetrack aimlessly? telling ~99.999,999 others to give up the race and go elsewhere to die? Or, after the placenta comes out after 9 months or so, had it become a graveyard for "dead slow swimmer sperm bodies" include those extras through extra efforts by dad of **IT**s until he realizes such efforts are not needed, or mom yells "STOP IT", *I am* already pregnant".

The writer cannot help but think of each sperm as a rejected person. Looking at it a different way, does the swim race for the loser sperms continue "till its death"? - all of them battering at the hardened egg shell in a manner resembling Alexander battering Tyre's walls for a couple of years? What does really happen in this ever-repeating drama in the next few seconds, minutes, or next hour? The writer really wants to know.

Consider everything inside your body (male or female). The movement of anything inside is confined one way or another! What does that mean? Blood flows *confined* through the blood-vessels; a hair's follicle grows out of the skin from its *confined* root. Air goes into the lungs and out, *confined t*o your nasal/mouth passages; food goes one way through a very long, complicated *confined* track. You get the point, right?

But not so with the sperms! When released, they must move directionally with a mission. Question: are the new sperms restlessly swimming within ever-ready semen in the testicles? The writer's limited knowledge points to a no. That means the 100+ million restless sperms (each may be screaming like a cicada, "Get me outta here, please, I have an important date") get thrown into a viscous swimming medium for the first time in an ejaculation to bang against a vaginal wall.

Just imagine this: the entire fleets of all the coastal European countries vying for supremacy along the North Sea coasts being toppled over due to severe North Atlantic weather. The fallen homo-sapiens from the ships have a better chance of survival because their bodies have limbs so they can swim ashore.

Not so the sperms thrown into semen because it has merely a tail. A sperm wouldn't make out the "heads and tails (!)" of directions to go the right way to meet the egg. For any one right direction, there are a hundred wrong directions. Call them forks in the road. They may all follow the erring leader and head the wrong way. Oops, no play ball or pregnancy this time.

Section 9: The Odds of the Two Halves Meeting

The egg knows how to discard itself from waiting if it has been "stood up" for long enough. It does not go back in and come back out to give a second chance to anyone. It exits the body with a big show-and-tell. If you pay attention to the normal parts of one's body, such as the eye, the tongue, the arm, the stomach, etc., you will notice each needs a signal from your brain to do anything that requires any movement from that part of the body. There is constant feedback between the brain and the body part ordered to make physical the move just as ordered from regions 1 and 2 of the brain, illustration 13.

But the tiny, tiny single-celled, tail-wagging half homo-sapien swimmer-sperms from a future daddy not only seem to know for themselves where to go to poke a hole in "the egg" *if the she-half is there* in waiting, In addition, the single-celled half-homo-sapien mama egg seems to know the instant when it should clamp self's wall like a fortress against the penetrant and not let his tail get in, in addition to not letting any other sperm poke in. Occasionally, a second sperm, and very rarely a third, make it through the egg's wall. Must be a photo-finish. Two sperms get into one egg, and we have so-called identical twins, - the writer was told. But no two twins are really strictly identical. The half-male sperms were not identical to begin with, even if they share the same female half. Hypothetically, if every one of the sperms in the vaginal tract mated with the same egg *separately*, or each sperm mated with a different egg if at all possible, we would have different homo-sapiens with slightly different looks and very different temperaments conceived, each as a full male or a full female homo-sapien. Mind-boggling situations of odds come into play here. No one gives a heck about any of the half homo-sapiens if there was no conception "Let them die", but if the half female egg is being discarded, it is a big deal of show and tell! (in the writer's household, customarily the woman sits out by herself for 3 to five days and none of us are to touch her until she states "all clear".

Once again, it is the female that gets all the attention. But should the halves meet and get bonded, the combo immediately starts dividing, forming a new homo-sapien in matter of time. It is the start of a pandemonium inside and outside the homo-sapien mother's body. You won't believe the rate at which the conceived whole cell starts dividing. It is comparable to Lucille Ball facing the oncoming chocolates on the conveyor.

Millions of the late swimmer sperm worms seem to simply perish, never to be heard of again or given another chance, as if anyone cares. No one living in droves gets rejected so horribly so often. The writer wonders if this attitude is present in the real outside world, too. This may sound sexist, but in the outside world it's the male who goes to pick her up, but it's the lady who is almost never ready! Of course, the sperm is not a destroyer of anything but a builder. Compare them to white blood cells; the leukocyte finds bad guys *on its own* in the body and gives each a bear hug of death The winning sperm finds the waiting egg *on its own but gives a poke of love*. But unlike sperms, each leukocyte does not have to be unique!

Do the sperms and female eggs must have their own independent intelligences regarding how to behave towards each other and how to behave together thereafter? Until a full brain grows for them, each one's DNA seems to be each one's half brain.

This writer now will narrate the biography of an important and influential person in the writer's life. Upon insistence by the writer, *he* finally wrote *his* growing up story for posterity.

It appears from his writings he really must have wanted to do **IT**, once he was mature, and which teenager does not want to? Different cultures, different faiths, different restrictions, and different taboos about doing **IT,** if one feels it **and** likes **IT**! The itch to do **IT** is all the same, regardless of cultures, religions, restrictions, and taboos. (The writer could not stop laughing when he read about one who decided to become a preacher very early on, joined a seminary early to spend his whole life, and upon puberty and then onwards not being allowed to be anywhere close to the opposite sex, did **IT** about 20 times a day into open air just to relieve self of the uncontrollable itches. For *god's sake*, he surely chose the wrong profession, just to make his parents proud, not knowing what the itch for **IT** would be like.)

Till now, all his (the writer of the biography) urges could have been going up very privately into the open air just like the guy who joined the seminary! He was an orphan for most of his life, and that the writer knew. He does not remember seeing his dad; and he barely remembers his mom. Both died even before he reached five. He often repeated that to this writer, "I do recall her face as she lived till I was four," but he doesn't recall dad because he died too early. (Soooooo sad! *This writer feels deeply* for anyone who came into this world but whose pa or ma, or both, died so early that the kids cannot recall seeing them or doing anything with them. Fortunately, this writer had full emotional contact with mom and dad till they died, but not always kosher)

After he became an orphan, the chosen kith and kin *who were entrusted to raise him* and also his older sister and the oldest, a brother— just as in any normal history for foster parenting goes, - they gnawed gradually at the orphans' sizable inheritance, *much more than they should have*. The three siblings—himself, his older brother, and older sister—all orphaned, had to be taken care of till they could take care of themselves. Who is going to blame the

THE KITH AND KIN OF HANUMAAN

caretakers when the excuse was they were taking care of three young kids, with the oldest boy being barely ten and an orphan? But the younger lad was young, handsome (the writer knows this!), intelligent—and most importantly, *of the desirable type*. Even if poor now and an orphan, he had all the other qualities needed by those who were responsible for selecting him for the biggest task of their responsibility, i.e. tying his life to someone else's life.

Additionally, he had all the needed credentials: he spoke their desired language's ethnic *high-level lingo*, was from the very adjacent town, was of the same ethnicity, was of course of the same religion, and had two years of college to boot. So, they chose *her* for him, and he hinted he was ready for her (and secretly to do **IT** in real). No more of the thin air claiming all his production, day in and day out. But the elders insisted, you may be 18, but she is only 12, so you have to wait and lead a separate life until she is at least 16. That is the rule. Also, the law won't allow her to be a part of your life at such a young age. Claim her pre-puberty, *but wait till we say it is OK for you to do* **IT**!

And he obediently waited four years to pair up with her and dad got his chance to do **IT** in the real way. His brother and sister were already coupled up with their own partners a while back, and finally taking care of the youngest must have been a real relief for their caretakers. It seems the elders had done their final job only after chipping away at a major chunk of the siblings" inheritance, leaving all three relatively penurious. The result of this pairing up was the appearance of the writer into this world after the birth of his two brothers and a sister.

There may be over 2.5 billion sperm-producing homo-sapiens at this very moment on this planet, and the sperms each male produces for each ejaculation are in the range of 100+ million. 385,000 babies are born each day. You can AI-Google it. 2,500,000,000 x 100,000,000 minus 385,000 = you do the calculations = sperms **simply junked today**! No one knew of these types of facts and numbers until a few hundred years ago. Our ancients were great people as far back as we can go, but honestly, they knew zilch about many of the microscopic phenomena going on in any mammal. Today, now, we can record any facts and videos accurately digitally forever to be available.

Now let us come to the homo-sapien mama's side, who may not be that generous and wasteful, but still, she harbors about 400,000 eggs in total *for life* since her birth. The Eggs are ready after her puberty, but she releases a measly single egg once every ~28 days (like as though, she is going live for 400.000/12=33,3333 years…daaah!). That too, she offers the measly egg for the "play-ball" period for just a few measly days of the "single 28 day recurring period game". We may not know which egg in the 400,000 eggs mama will let slip out in wait for our finalist champion swimmer sperm, because genetically each egg is supposed to be unique by DNA. We do not know which champion swimmer sperm-worm will get the penetrating burst of hug, kiss, and making out because each sperm is unique too. The odds now are 292 billion x 400,000 = 116.8 billion-billions, or ~117 trillion, and the auto-biographer waited eight years post-puberty, *since he started production of the wigglers* for something to happen inside his new bride's....

(Warning: after the above math, the writer is not going to do any more calculations. *You do the math if you are so interested!* If the writer's math could be wrong as much by 50%, and forgive him because he is simply tired of correcting constantly the numbers. Know that we are talking odds of hundreds of millions of sperms at the smallest to trillions at the highest and so Go figure yourself if you want real accuracy!)

Let us look at some other odds that can enter the picture, but we will not do any more mind-twisting math. A reminder that the parents of this winning homo sapien sperm and the parents of the trophy egg carrier also went through their own births *through similar odds* and finally came to their conception we are interested in talking about. Looking at odds this way, - one can keep going backwards into grandparents and further back beyond. *One little deviation somewhere* means a different homo-sapien other than you would be present for this writer, or no writer would be available to write this write-up for you to read. But, we both made it Did you grasp the odds through which you and this male homo-sapien writer made it into this world to this stage of finally meeting through this write-up? How cool or hot is it that you and this writer made it? **Are you getting the idea that nature is basically a real killer of millions just for the birth of one?** In evolution with natural selection added in, as is the case, the odds of creating an offspring get worse still! Not every male is *given* a chance to do **IT**, and so billions of sperms get simply wasted away.

Uyyay-yayyay-yay (the reader is supposed to look down and shake the head left to right every time he says the words over and over)

I wonder if this killing attitude of nature is what we homo-sapiens carry on outside too—the eagerness to kill others of our own type for frivolous reasons.

Change the direction and look forward; the continuing process of being born into this world clean, still has odds against for both of us. The odds and calculations are not over yet! Both the hosting mama and the successfully mated two halves inside her womb must hang around as a healthy threesome union for about nine months. This is a very delicate, albeit perfectly natural duration indeed. Even with today's help in health, 1 in 175 does not make it outside alive to be a writer or a reader. That figure is for homo-sapiens. Other animal mammals have their odds too. But tadaaah! This writer made it after about nine months in a tough but cozy confined to at-home delivery bedroom. So did you, probably in much better circumstances at a nice hospital. As was handed down to him for his own to occupy, under the rights and privileges of a newborn, he was often in someone's soft *arms a lot or on a tiny piece of real estate—a flat ceramic-tiled floor, next to mama.* This is where he was to lay for several years until he was weaned away. He remembers mama rejecting his accustomed advances. Sooooo, he slept for 18 years on the same bare stone floor with little extra tile space granted at each growth spurt. The writer got his first comfy 2" thick bedbug-laden mattress only after he went to college at age 18.

At home, as the youngest, he had normally slept in between mom and dad "for many years," a lot closer to mom and clutching her toe length clothing as a small boy, with one hand and nursing the other opposed thumb between his lips (for future writing?). No younger sibling was ever conceived, and the writer seems to know the reason as to "why there could not be anyone coming anymore!"

With barely open sleepy eyes, this is what happened one night that he watched through a half millimeter slit between his eyelids. Here was the scene for a brief period of maybe five seconds. In that crowded 10" x 10" room where all six of us slept on the ceramic tiles, though too young to understand and not fully asleep yet, the writer recalls clearly dad's arm reaching mama subtly over him, and then squeezing the flesh on mom's buttocks. In a minuscule of a second, tiny mom's palm grabbed dad's fat wrist and flung it away with all the energy it had. To this day, the writer can recall "the loud thud" from dad's hand crashing on the opposite adobe wall. *That was it*—the end of anymore **ITs**; no more "a dad sperm will meet a mama egg" encounter ever again to happen in that room or anywhere else between those two.

There are about 23 million miscarriages annually globally, or 44 as a minute goes by. You and this writer made it past facing those odds too. Coming out into the real world presents a full day or more of drama and danger, danger for not one but both the homo-sapiens. Then, there are situations where the child or mama dies during the birthing process. Imagine all the homo-whatevers dying on the day of birth or anytime during the incubation period for the past six million years, whose fertile sperm-egg combinations could have had descendant homo-sapiens in today's world! *Again,* **is more of a killer than a miracle worker.** There are stillbirths that increase the odds of being born, but enough of these grim statistics.

Section 10: The Two + Two = Four Types of Big-Bullies

For 6m+ years the biped, the hominin, the homo-sapien has always been forced to stay under the thumbs of the muscular big-bully. That was the route set by the chimp-chiefs with no choices or extra women given to other male chimps. To that gets added next at some undetermined time, is the religious holy-man who also does become eventually a big-bully, controlling the faith-based supernaturalism of large groups. Then in the modern days came added "the extremely rich" big-bully, and the elected or otherwise "political" big-bully. All these four types have continued to misuse the common homo-sapien and the environment of the earth, doing so even to this day. Go too far in such misuse and they may create the atmosphere akin to the sort of "French, Russian, American, and 1848 type revolutions".

Right of the bat: The muscular big-bully, as he descended down from the chimp and mammals before, is almost already the foremost bully for his group, an had been so for eons. He always possessed the latest greatest killing tools no matter who developed them. Consequentially as the tools got better the actual muscle power required by him became inconsequential. His groups ordinary members were never allowed to have any of the killing tools until their allegiance was certain.

(It is interesting terminology that the big-bully holy-man's preaching often used the hallucinated phrase *kingdom* of heaven. Must have started after muscular big bullies called themselves to be kings, and sometime later they did shake hands with the growing influential religious big-bullies)

Some political systems will legally facilitate any member of homo-sapiens to become ultra-rich, *and that is fine*. But that appears to also create the 3rd type ultra-rich-bully and allow them to squander precious resources to satisfy their egos, - the misuse and overuse of earth's resources. *Private* personal rocket launches to name one misuse, and there are other misuses the ultra-rich favor. Their greed for riches and their ego contributes to many of today's problems of the environment.

For the longest time, the big-muscled big-bully homo-whatever subjugated, controlled, and directed large numbers of homo-*whatevers*. Then came into being separately, the so-called holy-man, who was able to influence individual homo-*whatever* members regardless of which big-bully group they belonged to through his charismatic *thinking*. These homo-whatevers thus influenced could have belonged to several neighboring groups, probably aggravating the controls set by the respective muscular big-bullies.

The holy-man's influence on the members of various groups—those who had now become conscious of having a fear of their death and the new concepts of salvation, afterlife, and such—had become airtight and perpetuating.

The muscular big-bully had been graduating into becoming a king with a kingdom. ***All kings, big and small, are descendants of muscular big-bullies.*** Soooooo, Ordinary homo-whatever members gradually faced two big-bullies:

- One was royalty,

- The other was a preacher. And this went on for sometime

Bottom line: According to the writer, all kings and their descendants were trained to be big-bullies deep at heart right from get-go, even if they behaved largely as great peace-loving homo-sapiens. Taking care of their subjects under a fist or swords was their duty. Modern times are full of these handshakes between the religious big-bully, the royal big-bully, the rich big-bully and the Political Big-bully. All of the four bullies exploit all the others under their thumbs.

Unbelievable amount of effort has been exerted in the creation of large edifices erected to the memory of big-bullies for thousands of years. During The Evolutionary

Modern Times, just picture all the slaves along up and down the Nile River of Africa who struggled on and on to build those huge obelisks, pyramids, and half homo-sapien, half animal-like sphinx structures, just for the afterlife of one big-bully after another. The religious big-bullies stood by constantly bossing over the slaves.

We are taught to revel in the lives of those mummified big-bullies, with barely a footnote to think about the slaves they harbored or ***the killings they performed***. Someone there who died in such misery could have been the reader's direct ancestor, and here if that is so, you have been trained to admire his killer bosses! Our brains by then had already grown in size to that of present day's size, but the use of it or the knowledge of its existence was severely controlled by the big -bullies. Neither the serf nor the slave knew he already had big brains.

Even at this present day, we are trained very early to revere how great the big-bullies were and still are. ***Shame on perpetuating such teaching values***. As history it is OK, but as a value, it is outdated.

This process of always innovating better tool had to do with a look at the growing brain's *options*, call them tines of a fork, of which intelligence (thinking, hallucinating) for more muscle power with better nutrition and tool use are only just a few. The natural leaning for homo-sapiens was always towards muscle power benefitting the big-bully, and the other tine leading to think more deeply into *what a homo-sapien should become* through non-violence and compassion was probably not realized. The dominant muscular big-bully must have clamped down on any changes in attitude other than obedience. As late as 80 to 100 years ago one famous Russian succeeded in killing millions of homo-sapiens of whom he thought that their mere intellect made him unsure of his big-bulliness.

Homo-*whatevers* evolved into deeper reasons to misuse the power of their incessantly expanding brain. Blame it on genetic mutation of the growing brain trying to figure out what else it can think that can complicate further a homo-sapien's life. It developed feelings of ego, pride, superiority, inferiority, anger, hate, prejudices, jealousy, and more qualities within its kind. In what order all these developed may be impossible to figure.

All primate species have their muscular big-bullies with various temperaments and social interactions with the stooges who hang around forming the group; many stooges may want to compete for sexual dominance as well. Still, natural selection is a pyramid scheme favoring the muscular big-bully until he gets too old and weak. If he has not set up a capable descendant in time, another random muscular big-bully might take over thus starting a new lineage. As the bipeds evolved into homo-whatevers, they transformed the moderate big-bulliness of chimps into a world of different order of cruelty. The big-bully was always male. For the past 6 million years, there have always been big-bullies among the species changing into various homo-*whatevers*, and studying the last 5,000 years the records of which are available in this write-up, they seem to have gotten worse and crueler, *killing their own kind for many and any reasons.* The descendants of bipeds kill their own kind just to maintain dominance.

The young descendants of muscular big-bullies, along with their close-knit homo-*whatevers*, may have witnessed routine violence by their group's big-bully. Being in constant proximity and companionship with related homo-whatevers and constant violence, they absorb the need and methods of *killing other competitors as a routine.* Such violence became a part of homo-whatever culture, that followed the tine of **killing for dominance** of the options fork.

The inherited animalistic system from chimps facilitated the muscular big-bullies to control ever-enlarging groups of homo-*whatevers*. As their groups became larger, they tended to be *upgraded into so called "kings"*. **All kings" ancestors were pure big-bullies at some stage.** The certainty of the extra region of the brain of a big-bully might have facilitated his tactics in being the first to use new killing tools to intimidate all group members, no matter who was clever enough to develop the tools.

THE KITH AND KIN OF HANUMAAN

As we approach The Evolutionary Modern Era with big-bullies having control over larger groups, *these kings got upgraded to royalty*. With the allegiance of different kings and royalties, we can say the creative homo-whatever created the position of an emperor. We cannot be exactly sure when all these complex transformations took place, but the writer suspects they were initiated by the onset of continued increase in brain size from, say 1200cc.

This handshake agreement between the first two types of big-bullies to evolve culminated in such misery for the commoners that we can peer through revolutions that took place in many regions concurrently, in the recent past of 115 years ago called "the Great War". The growth of the brain is the chief silent architect in the creation of all fabricated concepts and beliefs in **god-etc.**, and supernatural entrapments. The onset of French and Russian revolutions are clear examples of the cruel handshakes between the big-bully types.

The homo-sapiens of The Evolutionary Modern Era, when they had no explanation for what was happening after **IT** took place between a female and a male, *they credited the happenings to **god-etc.**,* Some even concocted births happening without **IT** happening. Among some, beliefs lead to special homo-sapiens being born without conception which of course is pure deception. A birth never takes place due to just one homo-sapien, it can happen only after a mother is coupled through **IT** with the father. Absolutely no IVF or petri dish conceptions that long ago.

This meek octogenarian writer has been raised in an atmosphere of 100% non-violence coupled with 100% pacifism for 100% of his growing days. No matter how aggressive and crude he may come across at times in this write-up, it is by and large so as to entertain and inform the reader. **His underlying theme is always malice towards no one,** *but not necessarily charity towards everyone*. The homo-sapien's ego does need punishment often, *often,* **often** enough.

Big-bullies, first the existential muscular type, and later the holy-man bully pulpit type creating **god-etc**. from thin air must not have had their separate ways influencing without any handshakes, for a while. Where and when this new supernatural philosophy through two combined big-bullies started, we cannot be exactly sure.

But the hectic homo-sapien activities on faiths, before the so-called "The Evolutionary Modern Era" (i.e., before the past 10,000 years) appears to have taken place in regions near *Sinai, the Levant, the Caucasus, Anatolia, Mesopotamia, Persia, etc.* We cannot take our focus away from these regions as the radiating influences for the births of variety of religions. It appears the lives and ignorance of the general normal homo-sapiens must have been so messy that they must have welcomed *any sort of a messiah's message to soothe them*. On one side the Muscular big bully completely subjugated them, on the other side their grown brains *told them silently* that they ought to have more freedom. It is not that difficult to create "a god" out of thin air and give him all the credit for the complex process of birth, then blame ourselves for all sorts of imagined sins and wrong doings. But today? Do we need such baseless thin-air-created beliefs?

Those ancient times should have been the tail end, the culmination of the ignorance of homo-sapiens taking the wrong direction with their enlarged brains, into the direction of full ego, greed, hate, bigotry, and ignorance. If we go back 10,000 years or more even, before The Evolutionary Modern Era (10k), **our brains then were just as big as they are today**, maybe mere 1 or 2 cc smaller. *Conclusion: we had as much intelligence then as homo-sapiens do today, and yet it is only recently that* **our brains really woke up** into investigative science. Can we blame the muscular big-bully for keeping our curiosity under his thumbs all these years? Yes, *yes*, **yes**.

We could have taken the progressive direction of global peacefulness and cooperation **starting then**, *or even before*. But we were handicapped and trained to be violent and perpetually combative by those ego-bathed big-bullies. We have not fully graduated yet because we still maintain a fascination for them and are trained to emulate them.

To this day entertainment is not worth watching unless it involves unmentionable amounts of violence and ever creative killing tools. "I'll be back" is the admired motto, and so is 'kill them all'. By the modern politics of today, many of today's big-bullies are of a different type namely the third type, super-rich, possessing large egos as always. They have taken unique avenues to display their machoness. A few of these individuals with their resources send *a fully wasteful, fueled rocket into space,* and we are to admire it to no end.

Rather than them worry at least a teeny bit about the environment they are damaging, why not worry about how all the rivers in the world are washing away pristine fertile soil *forever to ocean's floor,* and why not devise methods prevent it by collecting it? - such soil which only nature can create is needed in many desert-type places *for homo-sapiens of the future.* This crème-de-crème soil, *once gone to the ocean's bottom is never to be available again.* Follow Colorado River as a guideline!

Then comes about a 4th type of big-bully, - the powerful political junky and a lobbyist selling self's or others" interests to other big-bullies. with no care on scrutinizing projects detriment to the environment with wasteful spending.

Know this: ***No one is going anywhere into space to colonize, at least for 1000 years but we can wreck our environment permanently in less than 50 years.***

In actuality, living simply today and fully *satisfied is unbelievably easy for anyone* in a halfway developed region of the earth, and no wasteful extravaganzas are needed. *Thank the scientists!*

There needs to be a system whereby any big-bully can have all the resources any political system allows, **but** he should not be allowed to wreck the environment. Give him incentives to enhance the environment.

We must create a system, where but for legitimate defense of an established working system, no big-bulliness should be allowed to exist. You the reader of today who enjoys good living with adequate accommodations and modern conveniences of health, food, and transportation, should realize that such a favored situation was made available for you only after unmentionable amount of violence and killings that took place *against the original native inhabitants* on the very real estate you occupy. Languages, cultures, civilizations, and many homo-sapiens have been destroyed in the process of unjust dominance which today is for your benefit. Let the homo-sapiens of today repay "the royal luxury of food, accommodations, health and leisurely activities" they enjoy ***by attending to the environment***. Trust the writer, no royalty in the past with his resources enjoyed as much luxury as you can with your resources today! Driving an allwheel drive for hours is easier than being saddle strapped for mere half hour.

Section 11: Consequences & Constancy of Brain Growth and The Awesome Foursome

Though other animals create sounds and seem to communicate things like danger and aggression, it does not appear that they are creating full sentences to describe situations. Animals do not seem to converse with each other but simply utter meaningful sounds between themselves. Our brain growth has given us unprecedented vocals as a side benefit.

The writer thinks the growing brain focused on the enhancement of vocal cords and opposed thumbs *in parallel* to when bipedalism was initiated. The evolution of the vocal cords and their use for language and singing must have also started several homo-*whatever* species ago.

Animals simply do not have our advanced vocal cords. Only the perennially growing homo-sapien's brain created the vocal cords, and all the muscles of the mouth and chest region to create the dozens of languages with thousands of sounds and accents we have. Add to that list, your favorite singer's singing. To the writer it was the effect the Fab-Four had with their Hard Day's Night, oh about 61 years ago. But the very concept of advancing rudimentary animalistic sounds into a complicated language involving verbs, nouns, adjectives, tenses, etc., to describe either the hallucinated afterlife or the true nature of the universe and nature through science, requires a very large space of the 3rd region of the brain.

Our growing brain seems to have had disproportionately accelerated skillfulness on opposed thumbs, vocal cords, and sexual behavior because the basics of sight, touch, hearing, and tasting are reasonably similar (or often inferior) to other mammals and chimps. In the few mentioned of the thumbs, and vocals we really excel.

Unless homo-sapiens of any particular language realize that *it is only the process of science which reveals life and the universe in a truer form with new needed words added,* **their language will die**. Languages even though esoteric, will not survive strictly based on art forms. Intra-interaction between homo-sapiens and interpretations of living culture can take beauty in a language and art *only so far and that will be it*. Any language that intensely focuses on science will never die because science by its very nature of trying to explain the universe creates new words, thus enhancing a language. **All dying languages note! Embrace science.**

Of course, a dominant homo-sapien group can simply kill all the other homo-sapiens speaking certain other languages but are less dominant, and unfortunately that is what has happened with so many Native American languages. An amazing example is the penguins" temporary habitat on the shores of Antarctica. The penguin baby, among thousands upon thousands, is recognized by the returning parent coming back from the sea after *hunting by sound and looks*. The baby penguin better stay put in place because if it wanders off and is not able to recognize its own meager square foot of space on its return, it is most likely doomed to death by the other adult penguins. What a cruel world.

Though for a mother animal it is easy to recognize its own baby separate from all the rest, for the father animal it is possible to recognize offspring *from his female but one that is not his*. Often if an offspring is born to his female by some other male, that infant's life could be doomed. Sexuality has such a hold on all mammals. Other than "us" the other creatures do not have any extra capacity in brain to "think through" such cruelty.

"Think for yourself, believe in yourself, have faith in your thoughts, trust thyself," etc., is a big misplaced "belief system" for the enlarged brain because such statements secretly hide beliefs in some sort of god-creator, subtly teaching you to mistrust others when you decided to be selfish with your efforts. Your thoughts and beliefs may be singularly yours but they are not at all connected to anything supernatural or other brains through some brain waves. Any apparent similarities between brains and thoughts are similar hallucinations based on similar upbringings in similarly hallucinated surroundings for creative thoughts.

"Trust thyself" is equivalent to "in making riches or trying to become a real winner, do not trust others", or on a killing field called warzone, rely on yourself and kill as many as you can. **Trust thyself is an extremely selfish big-bully attitude**, much admired and much misused. Hence, the forgoing statement is basically negative. No homo-sapien did anything worthwhile by being an island unto itself and trusting no one else. Trust thyself really means do not trust others, and a large group of individuals thus trained so create a mess through their belief systems. Since thinking happens in Region 3, one might as well think to say "don't trust others" as a routine advice for the faith based.

In its variation, the statement should be: think, think through whatever is urging you, verify in reality the benefits of your thinking as best as you can, have some trusted wise individuals check your thinking over, and in the end, if you think you are on the right path, go for your thinking. Because until some motion happens in the direction of your thinking, it is still your unproven hallucination, albeit one that might be or might not be worthwhile in the future. Much damage has been done by *stubborn individuals who trusted no one*, or did not learn how to develop trust.

Having been corrupted in various ways by beliefs and faith in the supernatural, with added negatives of false pride, hate, vengeance, a homo-sapien is unable to correct self fully, even when fully mature and having lived for a very long time knowing the damages caused by his beliefs in that "no use" super-natural environment.

The brain size growth into extra capacity *could have* transformed us into a very caring, decent, fair-minded, science-oriented society *right from the start*, but obviously, it did not. The muscular big-bully trait that we inherited must have always been the roadblock for any such change. But some region on the earth did transform their homo-sapiens" brains" functions into pacifistic ways, namely in the ancient Indian subcontinent.

The most rudimentary forms of the first religious supernatural beliefs likely started, maybe, in the N E corner of Africa, and then migrated to nearby regions, and then to the Far East, southern corner islands of Asia, Australia, interior ends of Africa, far eastern corners of Russia and all corners of both Americas. This seems to be precisely the reason why the far-off corners from the Levant regions seem to have the oldest primitive religious beliefs.

If you want to know *a modern verifiable true story* of a charismatic, wonderful individual who, the writer believes, *was in perpetual hallucination as to be living* **in the presence** *of his god of his belief,* google and read the life story of *Ramakrishna Paramahansa,* who lived about 160 years ago. He is a very well-known figure on the Indian subcontinent. His disciples and his relations felt, he looked as though he was in the presence of *his god (goddess!)* in real perpetuity, whether he was awake or asleep.

Per this writer, all of it must have been deep innocent hallucination because there is no such entity as god except in hallucination by an individual. His story depicts how the influence of parents" belief system inbred into him surely, is exponentially enhanced fully into a wholesome life when the surrounding influences also are *in full agreement with what he was raised with and feeling inside.* This is a great example of inbred religious faith further enhanced by believers of the same faith that surround the individual. This exceptional individual mentioned above was totally influenced without any internal conflicts or doubts about his desire to see his goddess. He appeared to be constantly in a trance and meditation all his life 24/7 for the physical appearance of his god-goddess in-person just as others around him were too but they were merely wishing.

He is extremely famous to this day among a very large group of homo-sapiens because of his own perennial personality in trance well described through records, *and also due to his obedient* **willing-to-be-celibate wife** with similar experiences as enthralled by him and constantly beside him. His enthralled pupils from his influences are also well known to too many millions to this day. *Such is the power of belief systems in god, though all of it is non-real and supernatural and nothing of that being real in the eyes of science.* It does bring forth the peacefulness and greatness in some individuals with none of any expected big-bully attitudes.

Give it all the credit, but then, blame it all also on the large brain too.

Soooooo…. a newborn baby, as it grows, is influenced by much more than what it is being taught vis-a-vis and how it is being lovingly handled at home. The child is also deeply influenced by all the sights and sounds surrounding it and the behavior of others in close proximity especially when such influences are in agreement with what is being taught at home. Ramakrishna Paramahansa was subjected to all such face to face and neighborly influences throughout his childhood.

Know Thyself? Trust yourself, Think for yourself are lousy, cheap statements when you look at them critically. They are supposed to be good advice when *you are seeking material gain* while encouraging you to trust no one implying that everyone else is out there to get you or pray for your failure but some god watching over you is going to assist you after recognizing your belief system in him. Baah humbug. Cultivate mentors and trust them too! Know the story of Olympian swimmer Phelps? The inherited muscular big-bully style behavior's enhancements went along for long periods as the brain grew, a few millions of years, with unawareness of a new process in opposition to it, that of camaraderie, non-violence, peaceful cooperation, etc. all also attributable to the increased brain space. But the existence of this extra brain capacity is not easily detectable by the child, especially when his caretakers, in an innocently ignorant way, are thwarting any mentoring in that direction due to their own limitations and deeply embedded preferences and prejudices. If not mentored or influenced to use fully all the smarts one does possess, right from the get-go of infancy, the individual will be at a disadvantage probably for all life—in a catch-22 situation.

Those that use their brain's extra space nearly to the fullest *are the ones you know about*, both on the hallucinated religious side, and also on the other of reasoning, science and engineering side. Many caretakers (almost always parents) start admiring their offspring only after he **shows the smarts on his own**. This is a huge common error on their part. *Every child needs to be* **deliberately** *mentored into smartness*. What is needed is a thorough pre-training of the caretakers themselves (most commonly parents) in an agreed, developed, professional way on how to mentor the child at every step *since birth* to realize the extra capacity given to him in the direction of freedoms through science and learn to recognize it as the extra capacity that grows with the child. All the while during mentoring, unconditional admiration, love, and protection should be given to him throughout, as the child's confidence in trusting what is imparted to him gets permanently established. Here mentoring alludes to training in natural processes and sciences *and not in supernatural beliefs.*

This mentioned professional pre-training of the caretakers is almost 100% absent. Based on one's ego and prejudices, a caretaker may reject any such training of mentoring his child, retorting to "nobody has to teach me how to raise my child". The writer is guilty of such braggadocio, through ignorance. Billions of others are too.

The writer trusts in this mutation of brain growth's permanence (existing in us even at present). It can decide the *intelligent use of the homo-sapien brain for the benefit of all humanity and the earth's future from deterioration* and destruction. Nine planets are circling the sun and none of them can claim even a small fraction of what we and the earth have.

Brain size and increased intelligence vary in homo-sapiens, one from the next as individuals and also as groups. The mistrust by a group against another group, is a complex emotions of group behavior indeed, and it is one of the several vexing features of homo-sapien living even after understanding the elimination of faith-based beliefs. The child's immediate and surrounding environment is also instrumental in the use of the extra capacity in region 3 to the highest levels of co-operation or to the lower levels of conflicts. The development of biases and prejudices by a homo-sapien within the self is a strong *"neighborly influence."* Said differently, a well-mentored child in Persia will be influenced largely by what happens around in and around Persia, and not by what happens in Greece or Egypt! Similarly, a child growing in Germany will be influenced by his Germanic surroundings in using his extra capacity and not by what is happening in, say, North Africa, and so on. Only when a child is mentored to be aware of this narrowness of influence does the child open up to better use of his extra brain capacity.

The following **Awesome-Foursome** are the most delightful results of the brain growth: they are not necessarily in order except for the 1st, since the order is uncertain:

1. Brain growth
2. Opposed thumbs
3. Bipedalism
4. Vocal cords

Please see illustration #1 for some perspective, that no other creature possesses these qualities in full bloom. The "awesome-foursome" really sets the pace for the extraordinary beauty in "us" as we selfishly see the beauty in ourselves proudly, and develop ourselves further to see beauty in innumerable other things. Why this awesomeness started with some selected chimps and not wolves, zebras, or some such mammal is a mystery.

Can you imagine horses imbued with such awesomeness to result in becoming "us" instead of primates, and we, in about 6 million years, standing 12 feet tall, weighing an average of 800 lbs., and being able to run 200-mile marathons? We would have no signs of having canines, and we all would remain vegetarians. Just a thought from the extra brain space, -why did we not evolve out of horses, **Mr. Ed**?

Using these large brains, the trend by a group of "us" to dominate over a different group of "us" has never stopped!

Portraying homo-sapiens as the chosen to dominate, and pointing to all the great things (technology, health, etc.) that we have accomplished makes us feel good *as of today*.

But the writer feels we have gone through a lot of sinister times in between these 6 million + the 10k years.

The first homo-whatevers to devise the better versions of weapons were almost always invulnerable to those that may have had the similar but somewhat inferior weapons. No hominin everywhere had the same quality of weapons at the same time, but all of them developed the same ego in application of them. There is no way to avoid variations in the superiority of groups among us goading many towards racial purity.

But the very desire to exploit that superiority in a dominating way **makes us less of who we are and what we can be.**

That extra brain space is very tricky indeed in also pointing out our deep faults and makes us insanely guilty. Muscularly, the bigger bullies always won over the smaller ones *and probably killed them*. That went way beyond the behavior of the original biped chimps in temperament.

The brain growth, always being the 1st anomaly, leaves the order of the other 3 in contention. Did the vocal cords and opposed thumbs already start evolving before the bipedal gene got established? There are many other awesome changes that made us finally homo-sapiens, especially in the field of sexual behavior.

Then come our face structure, flattening and the nose jutting out; - of course, the loss of the tail also.

Can you fathom the opposed thumbs" dexterity letting a surgeon do the most intricate surgeries on your body or an author writing a thick manuscript in any language? Consider the communicative and entertaining talents through our vocal cords; The sheer stamina our legs and bodies provide that can tire out any creature that dares to escape us. So many homo-sapiens routinely run 26.2 miles at the snap of fingers in about 3 hours? No

THE KITH AND KIN OF HANUMAAN

other living creature can do that. Researchers endlessly seem to talk of us becoming bipedal earlier than vocal, but this writer is unconvinced.

(You want to know the order of the awesome-foursome as based on the *ancestors of the Fab-Four?* Here is the dream wish of this writer.

Picture this as it might have happened 6 million years ago:

The "ancestors" of John, Paul, George and Ringo suddenly *showed up in the next tree belting out*, "She loves you yeah, yeah, yeah, she loves you...." followed by, "well shake it up, baby, now, twist and shout". and then "Hey you-oo-oo-oo, got that something, when I-yay-yay say that something, I think you'll understand" and many such others.

A full concert at the tree top followed while all four of them stood tall as bipeds on the tree branches, to the gasps of the first time onlookers in all the surrounding trees. Three in the band were deftly using opposed thumbs and stick-picks on stretched twines of trees on pieces of wood and the 4th cleverly holding sizeable sticks and banging harmoniously on the tree trunk. *The chimps in surrounding trees had never heard such vocals and percussion and **they just went crazy**.*

All the teenage chimps on the trees got so excited with this new music that they let go of the branches, started grabbing and poking their genitals in excitement and started jerking off in a frenzy while yelling and crying out tears (just like 63 years ago), a superb fore-runner for future performances for the London, Liverpool and Ed Sullivan shows! The result? They lost their grips on the branches and fell down to the ground. The teens stood on their hind twos and continued doing their lewd acts with their opposed thumbs and fingers while screaming.

There you have the beginnings of all four of awesome-foursome all at the same time, and so the writer dreams: The enlarging brain conceived great music, full use of vocal cords was initiated, while the band standing on their two limbs, and the finest use of opposed thumbs on strings was displayed. It was the real beginning of bipedalism and the indication that the opposed thumbs will be needed for *peaceful pleasures*, not just to make spearheads and arrows, and so the writer dreams!)

After that silly self-serving narration by the writer, let the researchers evaluate how the vocals of a great singer like Paul could go into over 3 octaves and combine with another great singer like John with his pleasing raspy tone. "Help me" understand and compare how the sounds of the Fab-Four evolved from the unbearable screeches of chimps. Would you believe, - that your bones, muscles, nerves, fluids in your chest, throat, mouth, tongue, cheeks, teeth, and lips, etc., coordinate with each other in immeasurable precision of movements and timing,

- to create, a mere lowering of ~8% pressure difference within your chest cavity against the ambient,

- and that creates all the extraordinarily meaningful talking,

- *in your own unique voice?*

- how about that some extra-ordinary singing coming out of you?

Talk, and the controlled sound-making is an "exhaling" process! No other creature comes even close to our talent, no matter how kindly we admire their efforts.

The skills and uses of the opposed thumbs for sexual pleasures of either male or female have already been noted. Though chimps and bonobos have opposed thumbs (two more than our two), they do not use them in any sexual acts; those *dumb bastards* don't realize what they are missing. No non-primate mammal can rotate any one of their four limbs enough to even touch their own or their sexual partner's genitals—in a gentle manner, of course. Maybe our poorer eyesight became so because there was no need to stare at those ugly pink female butts. Have you been to a modern gym lately? The writer has yet to see a male homo-sapien sitting at *a butt-tightening machine* which only females seem to use with their obscene "do **IT** now" type gestures of thighs swinging in and out. Every answer brings in a new question. Why did the pink butts stop appearing during ovulation invitations for female homo-sapiens? Further, maybe our poorer hearing became dulled after "marriages" got established as "the forever events" and one partner couldn't stand the other partner talking non-stop. Most animals don't follow any forever rules.

Assume three homo-whatever species—X, Y, and Z—*are living concurrently* all over the world. Species Y is a bit inferior to Z, and species X is inferior to species Y. Assume sexually, males of all three can interact with females of all three. If so, the writer believes that the homo-whatever-Z species killed all the homo-whatever-Y and -X species males for dominance, their women, and food. Such an elimination process, not existent among chimps, must have evolved into homo-sapiens to be the only to exist at some time by the end of the 6 million years.

Do you see how and why the brain size growth leading to newer, cleverer, and slightly more powerful homo-*whatevers* created easier situations for killing to the point of eliminating the previous inferior homo-whatevers? This killing spree must have been going on for hundreds of thousands of years among homo-*whatevers* until a threshold brain size was reached that created in addition deeper feelings of love, guilt, right versus wrong in relation to salvation, and recognition of male-female-kid as family. Brain growth in size is a biological process in evolution providing multiple usage options from region 3 for the hominin, but by the easier path of use it can be devious through hallucination, favoring violence, aggression, *killing for dominance.*

Homo-sapiens with larger brains and big-bully attitudes towards food, territory, and women, while constantly improving better tools, killed all the other homo-*whatever* as and when they encountered them. To this day, racial motivations are present, and they are easily noticeable, and those *can* lead to tendencies of attempts to kill all others or enslaving. *Love was and is always bigoted, but peace and non-violence are absolute.*

Bottom line: The idea that we evolved and were not created is today well established. *Nobody would dare teach you creationism* in any accredited school, college, or university *anywhere in the world.*

No amount of prayer will cure any sick person, only good medical attention will help. Proper care through modern medical establishments and proper personal medical care gives much better chances. No person that the writer knows even remotely relies solely on prayer and ritual to be cured when superb medical establishments are readily available within affordable reach. If one is brave enough to *really believe in their religious belief systems that credits the existence of a creator,* then would they boldly agree to teach their kids such beliefs starting from the time they reach 8 years, but not between 0 to 6 years as it is now? Teach them secular subjects till they are 8, since those are most important for full future living *with a job,* and teach belief systems however long needed after. For their 0 to 8 years, we can create *a well-thought-out, agreeable curriculum* of science and math. This curriculum of science and reasoning can be adjusted to the infant-child's first few years and his caretakers" temperament and then go pro. Do not forget! Mozart learned violin because his father was deep into that subject. By 5 or 6, he became a virtuoso. Such training today, *devoid of faith beliefs*, must start at infancy. It will take immense courage on parents" part to agree to any of this. But they need to raise their offspring in the most appropriate manner and least hypocritical manner, don't they!

Only we homo-sapiens can "act disingenuous." For animals, the truth is an open enactment. No dog comes to you with a wagging tail, licks you on your face, and then bites you.

How and when is it that we started getting these unique looks—say, like the looks of Semitic, Indian, Iranian, Chinese, Franco-Germanic, Slavic, Mongolian, African, and many others? As for the body's hair loss, that must have started genetically almost as soon as we became bipeds. The constant killing between groups explains all situations in other ways. Only the surviving group's characters will prevail

After a million years of zigzag backtracking migration, if hair loss started at a later stage, some place somewhere, then all homo-whatevers who have walked away in several directions would not all be subjected to hair loss and we should as a result see wide variations in body hair. The flattening of the chimp face and protruding nose must have also started almost immediately with bipedalism, unless we apply **the "kill them all" scenario** as explained above. In such case only the last species of homo-sapien succeeded traveling all over all lands and killed all others.

If one accepts that a continuous killing of inferior homo-*whatevers* went on *constantly,* then the question of when a certain physical change started is moot because all, everywhere, would have the features of the final victorious homo-*whatevers* at all locations as a finality.

If genetics is to be credited for our tribal looks, why do the homo-whatevers who must have wandered off in the same latitude not develop similar facial changes? Looking at the latitude passing through ~ the top of the Caspian or Black Seas, east - west, there are thousands upon thousands of unimpeded miles of land to migrate across and all hominins nearby this latitude *should look the same but it does not appear so.* The differences in the looks of homo-sapien tribes must have subtilties when compared to differences of looks in animals.

Homo-whatevers are capable of being insulted to their deepest core level, and such emotional turmoil does not exist in other mammals. Of the growing brain consider it as a fork a fork of two tines for the homo-*whatevers* to choose, one being the distrustful side qualities such as cheating, stealing, vanity, ego, pride, revenge, and hate; the other being what we will term as the benign tine of: kindness, love, compassion, innocence, protection of the weak, creative exploitation of natural resources, and so on. Until different tribes, with their determination to dominate, created artificial regions and boundaries (i.e., political), homo-sapiens were free to trek wherever and execute any action of their choice.

It appears that being able to study the available records of homo-sapiens in The Evolutionary Modern Era gives us a false impression of how great and advanced we are now, today. *The real narrative should be how bad we were for so long* and why we were not much better homo-sapiens earlier, say, since 10,000 to 5000 years before The Evolutionary Modern Era.

There are no science-based educators that ever resorted to violence in order to teach their methods, and it even sounds silly saying it.

There is *a region of variety of religions that never resorted to violence as a way of converting others to their way of life, namely the original Indian subcontinent.*

This region with no violence at core, simply offered a preferential way of living with non-violence, albeit along with normal "dreamt-up" ways of rituals that are supernatural in nature. These benign belief systems did succeed in spreading their non-violent values, chants and rituals. Non-violence was practiced in this region for such a long time that they had no concept of creating barbaric invasions of any kind into any of their lands. Certain belief systems in this region goes even to the extent of protecting the lives of germs and bugs by no breathing them in, by putting on a mask. Some of them wear perpetual masks not to protect themselves from germs but to protect the germs entering one's breathing system and be killed! The writer is pointing to the extreme right of Jain religion that originated in the Indian subcontinent, may be 4000 years ago.

Looking back, *it is appalling that the homo-sapiens paid that much attention to religion and never doubted that it was, and is, a complete waste of time and not needed for living a normal, decent truthful life.*

Section 12: Only "Us" to Remain, Kill All Others

(Hey Bungalow Bill, what did you kill, Bungalow Bill? - By the Fab-Four)

The resources available to different groups far and wide, existing geographical locations of various homo-sapiens in relation with access to water and food, access to weapons and their development, all such factors vary between groups gone far and wide innocently. Even if in the unlikely scenario that one group eliminates all other groups and has the entire earth for itself, the victorious group, given enough time, will evolve into various split groups and the meaningless need to kill-them-all will start all over again.

Any zigzag backtracking travelers considering themselves "superior and holy" homo-whatevers must have long ago either insisted that others (locals) convert to their new way of (religious) thinking, or they would be killed. This must have gone on most intensely for 5 or 10 thousand years before The Evolutionary Modern Era (10k years).

At the outset, it must be mentioned that though chimps appear peaceful, almost unlike other mammals, deep down, they harbor an immense capacity for violence, a tendency to kill their own kind in quarrels bordering on vengeance, and even cannibalism. This seems to happen between one chimp group and another. It might be worthwhile to remember this chimp behavior as we look into our own behavior as it got modified *and worsened* over 6m years.

The writer believes, sadly and sincerely that deep inside, some different groups of homo-sapiens even today, *if the opportunity arises*, would like to totally take over all other groups by killing or enslaving them. Such an attempt on a large scale took place during his own lifetime about 80 years ago!

Controlled enslaving was considered a useful option so as to have someone else to do all the master's chores while the master focuses on tasks that are not chores. Such enslavement, existed in some form throughout The Modern Era of Evolution. Constant slavery was most apparent for thousands of years along the Nile through the reigns of Egyptians and Nubians. The big bullies of then *of all types* seem to have thought nothing of it and considered it natural treatment of the subjugated homo-sapiens. Somehow this cruel concept got into some holy books (qitaabs) and so it has become the favored adherence of the faithful giving them legality to become cruel again!

Enslavement may come from the gratification needed for the big-bully's superego, forcing slaves to cut and drag for the new pyramids and obelisks huge building blocks. It is the glorification of the *life and death of a single big-bully at a time* based on supernatural beliefs, and such monumental tasks necessitated *slaves in huge numbers.*

The wrong direction taken by the growing brains, towards the newly evolved attitudes of greed, hate, machismo, and ego was predominantly ***"kill them all"***— kill those of our own type that we do not like and approve.

The right direction *could have been the attitude of curiosity* about nature and the persistent eagerness to learn all about this universe, which includes of course this earth also. Check for proof and evidence for anything found new. After all, that correct attitude is what we have gravitated to **now** starting with a few scientists of a few hundred years ago "with broad shoulders" as Newton would correctly quote. No one today dare seriously develop the horrendous attitudes of violence of a few groups as late as 85 years ago.

Alas, **after so much killing,** most of us seem to be on the right path, but we do not seem let our progeny be trained for that path until they are about six years of age. Until they become 6 and attend secular school, *we corrupt their learning in the wrong paths of supernaturalism,* and god-etc. attitudes. Only from age 6 onwards they enter secular schools to learn math and science to understand what looking for evidence is while examining nature. Notice why only homo-sapiens (us) remained and no other homo-whatevers, probably well before The Evolutionary Modern Era arrived. This is in spite of multiple bipedal species evolving into a dozen or so homo-whatever types from chimps of 6 million years ago. It is known that after the entire land masses of the earth were discovered by the superiorly tooled and adventurous Europeans of about 532 years ago, they found only homo-sapiens—i.e., us— existing everywhere they explored. Just imagine that not a single homo-penultimate or ante-penultimate of the homo-sapiens was discovered living anywhere in the world.

Is that not puzzling? What do you think might be the reasons? The writer's answer is that hominins are habituated to killing their own kind for almost any and sometimes the silliest reasons. Maybe, just maybe, among the millions of homo-whatevers killed in the Americas and down-under islands since about 532 years ago, some a few did belong to the penultimate homo-sapiens, probably Neanderthalensis. If we do have specimens of the remains of those killed long ago, we could have a more definitive answer through digging their graves up.

If one prefers to be pacifistic, peaceful, accommodating, and fair, and this tine on the options fork for the big brain is certainly possible, it is considered a weakness and is exploited immediately— by those muscular homo-sapiens tuned to wrong use of the extra brain space, from eons. As a reminder, one large homo-sapien group started the elimination process of whomever they deemed inferior only about 85 years ago under the leadership of just one deranged homo-sapien *and he almost succeeded.* No other creature has turned its living into such a zealous affair of killing every one of its own type or enslaving, that it determined the others to be different from it.

A major eruption of the kind of past mass killings is now unlikely because homo-sapiens are almost thoroughly getting intermixed gradually, and *too many know how to make weapons a billion times more dangerous than the swords and javelin spears of the times prior to The Evolutionary Modern Era.*

Some twenty-five or so years ago, this writer listened to a televised conversation between a western journalist and a Middle Eastern "very high-up" political leader (from the Levant region). What he heard shocked the writer, being totally unaccustomed to such utterances for violence from civilized people of today. Paraphrasing a bit on the journalist's question: "So, what do you propose the solution to be, Mr. so-and-so?" the journalist asked.

"**Kill them all**" was the un-hesitated reply of the political leader! *That leader is still living as a leader to this day.* This political leader is still high up today in regional politics, and the writer feels he still harbors such aggression though he no longer utters similar words. Though he may sound like he has toned down his rhetoric, this writer does not believe that deep inside him there is any change.

The strong feelings towards others by any individual or a group are generally directed toward proximate neighbors with whom the individual or group has constant visual contact to formulate biases and unfavorable feelings. "Kill thy neighbors" is probably a more apt sentiment harbored by some homo-sapiens more often than "love thy neighbors."

To his shock and amazement, this writer knows that the idea of the *political leader's proposed kill-them-all* was directed at a few millions of his immediate neighbors. Their numbers could have filled one or more modern urban cities!

The homo-sapien species—that is us—must have killed all the homo-*whatevers* that came before us, in a continuous chain of persistent killings of elimination. Will the reader have any doubts about that after looking at the extensive chart presented further below?

If you doubt the efficacy of this statement, just look at the plagiarized chart below. If we had more data, the chart could go back a few hundred thousand years. "Kill them all" is an attitude the hominin developed and maintained since eons.

A tabulation of **Killings** by homo-sapiens of homo-sapiens since ancient times, going back about 10k years.

It includes also **killings** of slaves by masters, but no deaths due to natural causes, such as disease, famine, etc.

(The following tabulation has been heavily plagiarized using data from Google search. W=War, CW=Civil War, k=1000, m=million)

#**Killings** Where, By **Killed** #s in **Killed Years ago Killed** locations & ref. row & Between **wars, battles from today**

1	All continents	100m+	2.6 k /10k	all over the world, *estimated*
2	Cyrus the Great	1m+	2564	Persian Empire & Middle East
3	Greco Vs Persian	300k+	2498	Greek Cites & Persian Empire
4	Chinese States	1,5m+	2372	7 great powers of China

5	Samnite W	34k+	2341	Roman Rep. vs. Samnites. Italy
6	Alexander	142k+	2304	Macedonia, Greece, Persia, M. East, & Asia,
7	1st Punic W	400k+	2277	Rome vs. Carthage
8	Qin's W	700K+	2250	Qin vs. Han Zhao Yan Wei Chu Qi States
9	2nd Punic W	770k+	2234	Rome vs. Carthage
10	Punic W	1.62m/ 1.92m+	2229	Rome vs. Carthage
11	3rd Punic W	450k/ 750k+	2172	Rome vs. Carthage, Tunisia
12	Cimbrian W	410k/ 650k 2131	2131	Teutones, Western Europe
13	Roman C W Actium	3m+	2085	Europe/North Africa/Middle East
14	Gallic W	1m+	2078	Roman Republic vs. Gallic tribes, France

15	Tigray W	162k/378k+	2021	UFEFCF /Ethiopian + Eritrean (Tigray, Afar, Amhara)
16	Iran–Iraq War	500k/1.5m	1984	Iran and allies vs. Iraq and allies
17	Iceni Revolt	150k+	1964	Roman Empire vs. Celtic tribes, England
18	1st Sudanese W	500k+	1960	Sudan vs. South Sudanese Rebels, Sudan
19	1st Jewish Roman W	250k/1.1m	1955	Roman Empire vs. Jews, Middle East
20	Jewish–Roman W	1.27m/2m	1923	Roman Empire vs. Jews, Middle East/ N Africa
21	Kitos War	440k+	1908	Roman Empire vs. Jews, S Europe / N Africa
22	Bar Kokhba Revolt	580k	1895	Roman Empire vs. Jews, Middle East
23	Wars of the 16 Kingdoms	150k+	1853	N Chinese States, Northern China

24	Yellow Turban Rebellion	3m/7m	1830	Peasants vs. Eastern Han China
25	Hunnic Reclaims	165k+	1800	Roman Empire vs. Hunnic Empire
26	3 Kingdoms War	36m/40m	1792	Wei vs. Shu vs. Wu China
27	Goguryeo–Sui W	300k+	1418	Sui dyn China, Goguryeo Kingdom Korea, China
28	Lushan Rebellion	13m/36m	1265	Tang dyn China and Islamic vs. Yan state
29	Arab–Byzantine W	2m+	1185	Byzantine Empire vs. Islamic Empire
30	Goryeo–Khitan Wars	90k+	1018	Liao Empire vs. Goryeo Kingdom of Korea
31	Song–Đại Việt war	600k+	948	Song vs. Dai Viet Kingdom China, Vietnam
32	Reconquista	7m	923	Christian/Muslim. Spanish, Portg Iberia

33	Crusades	1m/ 3m	831	Byzantine vs. Seljuq, Christians vs. Muslims.
34	Albigensian Crusade	200k/ 1m	806	Papal States and France vs. Cathar States, France
35	Mongol invasions	30m/ 40m	737	Mongol Emp vs. Eurasian states, Eurasia
36	Scottish Indndence	60k/ 150k	698	Scotland vs. England, Scotland / England
37	Conquests of Timur	8m/ 20m	637	Timurid Emp vs. middle eastern, Eurasia
38	100 Years" War	2.3m/ 3.5m	629	House of Valois vs. House of Plantagenet
39	Wars of the Roses	35k/ 105k	553	Houses of Lancaster, of Tudor vs. of York, Wales
40	Spanish / New Granada	8m+	505	Spanish vs. Colombian Colombia

41	Mediterranean War	900k/1m	502	Rep Venice, Spain, Genoa, Papal, Savoy, vs. Ottoman Emp
42	Spanish conquest of Mex	8m/10m+	500	Spanish Empire vs. Aztec Empire Mexico
43	German Peasants" War	100k+	500	German Peasants vs. Swabian League Germany
44	Italian Wars	300k/400k	499	Roman, Spain, Italy vs. France, Ottoman, etc., S Europe
45	Spanish / Nicaragua	575k+	495	Spanish vs. Indigenous peoples of Nicaragua
46	Campaigns of Suleiman	200k+	481	Ottoman vs.Balkan,African, Arabian,E Europe, M East,N Africa
47	Spanish / Inca Empire	8.4+	472	Spanish Empire vs. Inca Empire Peru

48	Spanish conquest/Yucatán	1.46m+	467	Spanish Empire vs. Mayan states North America
49	French W of Religion	2m/4m	444	Protestants vs. France vs. Catholics France
50	Anglo-Spanish War	106k+	430	Spanish vs. England, America, Netherlands, Belgium, France, etc.
51	Japanese / Korea	1m+	429	Kingdom of Great Joseon and Ming China vs. Japan Korea
52	9 Years" War (Ireland)	130k+	426	Irish rebels vs. Kingdom of England Ireland
53	Eighty Years" W	600k/700k	416	Dutch, England, France vs. Spanish, Northern Europe
54	Thirty Years" War	4m/12m	391	Austria +Spain vs. Anti-Habsburg states Europe
55	Wars of 3 Kingdoms	876k+	379	Royalists vs. Covenanters vs. Irish vs.

				Protestants, British Isles
56	English Civil War	212k+	378	Parliamentarians England, Scotland, and Ireland
57	Franco-Spanish War	200k+	377	France and allies vs. Spain and allies Western Europe
58	Ming to Qing	25m+	375	Qing China vs. Ming China vs. various peasant rebels China
59	Portuguese Restoration	80k	370	Portugal, France, and England vs. Spain Iberian Peninsula
60	5th Ottoman / Venetian	72k	367	Venice vs. Ottoman Empire, Candia, Crete, Dalmatia Aegean
61	Deluge	3m	366	Poland vs. Sweden and Russia Poland
62	Arauco War	125k/ 142k	354	Spanish Empire vs. Mapuches Chile
63	Franco-Dutch War	342k	349	France and allies vs. Dutch

				Republic and allies, W Europe
64	Mughal–Maratha	5m+	342	Maratha Empire vs. Mughal Empire India-Bangladesh
65	Great Turkish War	380k+	333	Ottoman Empire vs. European Holy League Eastern Europe
66	9 Years" War	680k+	332	France vs. Dutch, Habsburgs, England, Scotland, Spain etc.
67	Spanish Succession	400k/1.25m	317	Grand Alliance vs Bourbon Alliance Europe / Americas
68	Great Northern War	350k+	314	Russia and allies vs. Swedish Empire Eastern Europe
69	War of Jenkins" Ear	30k+	281	Spanish Empire vs. British Empire American South,
70	Maratha in Bengal	400k+	278	Maratha Empire vs. Nawab of

				Bengal India, Bangladesh
71	Seven Years" War	868k/ 1.4m	265	Great Britain and allies vs. France and allies Worldwide
72	Sino-Burmese	70k+	257	Burma vs. Qing China Southeast Asia
73	American Revolutionary	70k/ 116k	116k	United States and allies vs. British Empire and German
74	Tây Sơn rebellion	1.2m/ 2m+	238	TâySon, Chinese vs Nguyễn, Trịnh, Vietnam; Siam; Qing China;
75	White Lotus Rebellion	100k+	225	Qing China vs. White Lotus rebels China
76	Fr in Egypt and S Ymn	65k+	225	France vs. Ottoman, Great Britain, M East / N Africa
77	Snt-Domingue exp	135k+	222	France vs. Haiti and UK Haiti

78	Napoleonic Wars	35m/ 7m	215	Coalition powers vs. French + allies, Worldwide
79	Peninsular War	1m+	213	Spain, Portugal, UK vs. France, Kingdom of Italy, etc.
80	French invasion of Russia	540k+	212	French Empire vs. Russia Russia
81	Colombian W of Ind	250k/ 400k+	208	Royalists vs. Patriots, Colombia, Ecuador, Panamá, Venezuela
82	Venezuelan W of Ind	228k+	207	Spain vs. Venezuelan states Venezuela
83	Spanish Am w of ind	600k/ 1.2m+	204	Spain vs. American Independentists Americas
84	Mfecane	1m/ 2m	199	Ethnic communities in southern Africa, South Africa

85	Greek W of Ind	170k+	198	Greek Revolutionaries vs. Ottoman Empire, Greece
86	Carlist W	200k+	176	Carlist Insurgents vs. Spain, Spain
87	Crimean War	356/615K	170	Ottoman Emp + allies vs. Russia Crimean Peninsula
88	Taiping Rebellion	20K/70K	167	Qing China vs. Taiping Heavenly Kingdom China
89	Indian Rebellion	8K/1K	167	Sepoy Mutineers vs. British East India Company India
90	Punti–Hakka Clan Wars	5K/1m	163	Hakka vs. Punti China
91	French colonial campaigns	110K	162	France vs. Locals, Algeria, Tun, Morocco, French, etc.
92	Red Turban Rebellion	1m	161	Qing China vs. Red Turban rebels China

93	Miao Rebellion	4.9m	161	Qing China vs. Miao China
94	American Civil War	650K/1m	160	Union States vs. Confederate States USA
95	Panthay Rebellion	890K/1m	160	Qing China vs. Hui China
96	French in Mex	49K+	158	Mexican Republicans vs. France and Mexican Empire
97	French conq. of Algeria	596K	158	France vs. Algerian resistance Algeria
98	Austro-Prussian War	40K	158	Austrian states vs. German states Central Eu
99	Paraguayan War	300k/1.2m	157	Triple alliance vs. Paraguay South America
100	Dungan Revolt	8m/20m	155	Qing China vs. Hui vs. Kashgaria China
101	Franco-Prussian War	434+	154	France vs. German states France and Prussia

102	Ten Years" War	241k+	151	Spain vs. Cuba and Dominican volunteers [67] Cuba
103	Conq. of the Desert	30k/35k	147	Argentina vs. Mapuche people Patagonia
104	Aceh War	97k/107k	131	Kingdom of the Netherlands vs. Aceh Sultanate Indonesia
105	1st Sino–Japanese W	48k+	130	Qing China vs. Japan East Asia
106	Cuban W of Ind	362k+	128	USA and Cuba vs. Spain Cuba
107	W of Canudos	30K	128	First Brazilian Republic vs. Canudos inhabitants
108	Thousand Days" War	120k/180k+	124	Colombian Conservatives vs. Colombian Liberals

109	Boxer Rebellion	100k	124	Boxers vs. Foreign powers China
110	Second Boer W	73k–90k	124	UK+allies vs. S A Rep+ Orange Free State S
111	Russo-Japanese War	101k/206k+	120	Russia vs. Japan Northeast Asia
112	Philippine–American War	234k	119	Philippines vs. USA
113	1911 Revolution	220k	113	Qing China vs. Revolutionaries
114	Balkan Wars	140k+	112	Balkan wars/ Peninsula
115	Mexican Revolution	1m/3m	109	Pro-government vs. Anti-government Mexico
116	World War I	17m/40m	108	Allied vs. Central Powers, Worldwide

117	Russian CW	7m/ 12m	105	Red army vs. White army
118	Rif War	90k	101	Spain vs. Republic of the Rif, Morocco
119	2nd Italo-Senussi War	40k+	97	Italy vs. Senussi Order Libya
120	Chaco War	85k/ 130k	91	Bolivia vs. Paraguay, Gran Chaco
121	2nd Italo–Ethiopian W	278k+	89	Ethiopian Empire vs. Italy, Ethiopia
122	Spanish Civil W	500k/ 1m	87	Nationalists vs. Republicans, Spain
123	Chinese Civil War	8m/ 11.7m	86	ROC vs. PRC China
124	Winter War	154k/ 195k	85	Finland vs. Soviet Union, Finland

125	Greco-Italian W	27k+	84	Greece vs. Italy Southeast Europe
126	2nd Sino-Japanese W	20m/25m	83	Republic of China and allies vs. Japan, China
127	World War II	80m	83	Allied powers vs. Axis Powers, Worldwide
128	Continuation War	387k+	82	Finland and Germany vs. Soviet Union, N Europe
129	Soviet–Japanese W	33k/96k	79	Soviet Union and Mongolia vs. Japan, Manchuria
130	1st Indochina War	400k+	79	France vs. Việt Minh, Lao Assara, and Khmer Issarak
131	Greek Civil War	158k+	78	Greek Government army vs. DSE, Greece
132	Partition of India	200k/2m	77	India and Pakistan

133	Korean War	1.5m/ 4.5m	73	South Korea, allies vs. North Korea, allies, Korea
134	La Violencia	193k/ 300k	71	Colombian Conservative vs. Liberal Party
135	Annex Hyd	29k/ 242k	70	Dominion of India vs. Hyderabad
136	Algerian War	400k/ 1.5m	66	Algeria vs. France Algeria
137	Iraqi–Kurdish	139k/ 320k	64	Kurdistan/Iraqi Kurdistan+allies vs. Iraq +alliesIraq
138	Congo Crisis	100k+	62	DRC, USA, Belgium vs. Simba, Kwilu Rebels, Congo
139	Indnsian /E Timor	100k/ 200k	60	Indonesia vs. East Timor, East Timor
140	Vietnam War	1.3m/ 4.3m	59	Vietnam +allies vs. N Vietnam+ allies Vietnam

141	N Yemen C W	100k/ 200k	58	Yemen, Saudi Arbia vs. Yemen Arab Rep. UArab Rep. Yemen
142	Angolan W of Ind	100k/ 200k	57	Angola vs. Portugal and South Africa, Angola
143	Nigerian C W	1m/ 3m	56	Nigeria vs. Biafra Nigeria
144	Mozambican W Ind	64k/ 89k	53	FRELIMO vs. Portugal Mozambique
145	Kurdish sep. in Iran	15k/ 58k	53	Qajar dynasty vs. Shekak (tribe) Iran
146	Bangladesh Lib	400k/ 3.6m+	53	India and Bangladesh vs. Pakistan, Bangladesh
147	Kurdish– Turkish	100k+	52	Turkey vs. Kurdish people, Middle East
148	Ethnic/ Nagaland	34k+		India and Myanmar vs. Naga Peopl

149	Insurgency NE India	25k+	50	India and allies vs. Insurgent Groups
150	Colombian conflict	220k/ 450k+	50	Colombia + allies vs. Far Lft guerillas & Far Rgt paramilitary
151	S Afr inv of Angola	50k+	50	Cuba and MPLA vs. South Africa, FNLA, UNITA, Zaire, Angola
152	Afghanistan conflict	1.4m/ 2.5m	50	see Afghanistan conflict Afghanistan
153	Kurdish–Turkish conflict	45m	50	Turkey vs. KCK Middle East
154	Soviet–Afghan War	600k/ 2m	50	Soviet Union and Afghanistan vs. Insurgent groups Afghanistan
155	Salvadoran Civil War	70k/ 80k	50	El Salvador vs. FMLN El Salvador
156	Ogaden War	60k	45	Ethiopia and Cuba vs. Somalia Ethiopia

157	Ethiopian C W	500k/ 1.5m	42	Derg, PEDR, Cuba vs. Anti-Communist, Ethiopia
158	Arab–Israeli conflict	116k+	40	Arab Countries vs. Israel Middle East
159	Lebanese Civil War	120k/ 150k	40	Various groups Lebanon
160	Insurgency in Laos	100k+	40	Laos and Vietnam vs. "Secret army" and Hmong people Laos
161	Kashmir conflict	80k/ 110k	39	Pakistan, North India/ Pakistan
162	Conflict in Myanmar	130k/ 250k	38	Myanmar vs. Burmese Insurgent Groups, Myanmar
163	Internal conflict/ Peru	70k+	35	Peru vs. PCP-SL and MRTA, Peru

164	Ugandan Bush W	100k/500k	35	ULNF and Tanzania vs. National Resistance Army, Uganda
165	Moro conflict	120k+	30	Philippines vs. Jihadist Grps vs. Bangsamoro, Philippines
166	Angolan Civil War	504k+	30	MPLA and Cuba vs. UNITA and South Africa, Angola
167	2nd Sudanese CW	1m/2m	30	Sudan vs. South Sudanese rebels, Sudan
168	Somali C W	300k/500k	30	Varying Somali gov vs. insurgent groups, Somalia
169	Lords Resist Army	100k/500k	30	Lord's Resistance Army vs. Cl African st, Central Africa
170	Nagorno-Karabakh	50k+	30	Artsakh and Armenia vs. Azerbaijan + allies, Caucasus

171	Rwandan CW	500k/ 808k	30	Rwandan Patriotic Front rebel forces vs. Rwand QQQ
172	Iraqi uprisings	85k/ 235k	30	Iraq vs various rebels Iraq
173	Sierra Leone CW	50k/ 300k	30	see Sierra Leone Civil War, Sierra Leone
174	War on terror	272k/ 1.3m	30	Anti-Terrorist Forces vs. Terrorist groups, Worldwide
175	Communist rebellion	30k/ 43k	28	Philippines vs. Communist / Philippines
176	2nd Congo War	2.5m/ 5.4m	28	See Second Congo War, Central Africa
177	Ituri conflict	60k+	28	Lendu Tribe vs. Hemu Tribe and allies, Congo
178	Sri Lankan Civil War	80k/ 100k	25	Sri Lanka vs. Tamil Tigers, Sri Lanka

179	Gulf War	26k/41k	25	Iraq vs. Coalition Forces, Kuwait, Iraq, Saudi Arabia
180	Bosnian War	97k/105k	25	Bosnia, Herzegovinian gov, allies vs. Rep Srpska allies, Bosnia
181	Eritrean–Ethiopian W	70k/300k	25	Eritrean–Ethiopian War, Eritrean–Ethiopian border
182	Burundian CW	300k+	25	Burundi vs. Hutu rebels vs. Tutsi rebels Burundi
183	First Congo War	250k/800k	25	Zaire and allies vs. AFDL and allies, Congo
184	Algerian Civil War	44k/200k	20	Algeria vs. FIS loyalists vs. GIA Algeria
185	War in Afghanistan	212k+	20	War in Afghanistan (2001–2021), Afghanistan

186	Insurgency/ Maghreb	70k+	15	Maghreb, Algeria, Libya, Mali, Burkina Faso, Niger, Chad, Etc.
187	Iraq War (US lead)	405k/ 655k	15	Iraq War Iraq
188	War in Darfur	300k+	15	SRF and allies vs. Sudan and allies vs. UNAMID, Sudan
189	Kivu Conflict	100k+	15	see Kivu Conflict Congo
190	Khyber Pakhtunkhwa	47k/ 79k	15	Pakistan, USA, and UK vs. Terrorist groups, Pakistan
191	Mexican Drug W	200k/ 400k+	15	Mexi vs. Drug cart, inter-cartel conflicts, Mexico QQQ
192	Boko Haram Insurgency	350k+	15	Boko Haram, Nigeria/ Cameroon, Chad, Mali and Niger

1993	Libyan Crisis	30k/43k	15	Libyan Jamahiriya vs Anti-Gaddafi; jihadists in LIBYA
1994	Syrian civil war	507k/613k+	15	Syrian Arab vs. Rep Syria vs. ISIL vs. Syrian Dem, Syria
1995	Rojava–Islamist	50k+	15	Syrian Dem vs. Islamic St, Levant vs. al-Nusra Front., Syria
1996	South Sudanese Civil War	383k+	10	South Sudan vs. SPLM-IO, South Sudan
1997	War in Iraq	195k/200k+	10	Iraq and allies vs. ISIL Iraq
1998	Yemeni Civil War	377k+	10	Yemen. Hadi Gvt, + Saudi-led, UAE vs Al-Qaeda, YEMEN
1999	Myanmar Civil War	48k		Unity Gov vs. State Council, Myanmar

2 0 0	Rus. invasion of Ukraine	300k	5	Russia vs. Ukraine Ukraine
2 0 1	Hamas-Israel war	37k/ 45k+	2	Israel vs Hamas, Palestnns, Gaza Strip, W Bank, Lebanon, Syria

The most important item of above table is the estimations of numbers killed of homo-sapiens by homo-sapiens.

After browsing the above chart, are you still naïve enough to believe that the kill-kill-Kill'em-All desire within homo-sapiens is a myth? Above, do you see all the killings that occurred at the tail end (about 2,500 years before of today) of civilizations of Sumeria, Mesopotamia, Egypt, etc.? Killings are ongoing even today at this very minute in the names of dominance, race, religion, power, standard bigotry, etc.

The attitude to kill our own kind for various reasons has been instilled in many of us before we were barely 6 years of age. When we are taught how great a certain (our) warrior of past was, how he conquered so many places (=killed so many people) and became a great king or emperor. *Our innards are influenced permanently, constantly to equate killing as a great virtue.* Caesar, Genghis Khan, Napoleon, the Huns, and a few unmentionable individuals of very recent past—they all took advantage of the prevailing attitudes of the masses they impressed, beyond their own greed, **to kill, kill, kill.**

When will homo-sapiens realize that the earth has, its waters, its fluids, 100 or so elements really a *mingled ununiformly* on it, all of them needed for reasonable living? All those are to be harvested for benefit of homo-sapiens *through a reasonable formula of cooperation?* Moral and ethical values in this realm are simple common sense.

We even have the energy and technology to turn deserts into arable lands for future, but the compassionate will and understanding may be lacking. Anyone living today in an extremely comfortable real estate with all amenities *should remember that a lot of killing, displacing of other homo-sapiens probably took place at that very real estate under their feet* not too long ago by unreasonable homo-sapiens not bound by political rules. The Big-bully with a stick, arrow, sword, gun, or bomb was always the first divider and separator of neighborliness. Then shows up the religious, who ultimately does become a Big-bully also. He claims in finality the know-it-all attitude to know how to speak to god, a character he himself created out of thin air and never looked for evidence. ***Out of that original falsity is generated all other forms of other falsities*** of heaven, hell, miracle, reincarnation, soul, **god-etc.** - and the reader can create a few of his own. He must have scared the "heck" out of ordinary homo-sapiens who were just developing some deep concepts and fears about family living because their larger brains were urging them to think more subtly.

"After much suffering *much* under this king-cum-god *big-bullies* (name your places!!), common homo-sapiens rebelled to form new political systems, which created further new types of big-bullies who are neither kings nor gods but big-bullies nevertheless *with 1. - riches and 2. - political power*. Know more about Russian, French and such other revolutions.

As a pacifist, the symbols of the Eagle, Lion, etc., are actually hurtful and anathema to this writer, and such symbols will not be found with predominantly pacifistic homo-sapiens" ways of living, say in the large original Indian sub-continent. A leaf, a dove, a lamb, a cow—these are the preferred symbols by pacifists for peace, coexistence, and most importantly non-violence.

Did the penultimate homo-whatevers (Neanderthals?) and those just before them go through the emotional and physical turmoil of race, religion, ethnicity, etc. just like homo-sapiens do today, *now*? To the writer, it becomes obvious that once the concepts of god-etc. got established by, say, a few generations of mentors, a certain never-stopping zeal must have pervaded through the converts, urging the latest new converts to radially go out to kill or convert all of inferior quality homo-sapiens. In that respect comparatively, the zeal of the conquistadors of 532 years ago was puny and child's play. *No matter how great the faith is, it always matters who has the better weapons to kill* once the homo-sapien lingers on the muscular tine of the fork of options.

With bigger brains for everybody everywhere, each group on average has more intelligent members of different capacities and temperaments. Should they be creating varied forms of complexities of faith through hallucinating or straightforward reason and nature study through science?

Section 13: The Homo-sapien's Easiest Tasks: Thinking & Saying

The following are considered by millions to be the greats of history and their conquests have been well recorded: Darius, Alexander, Caesar, Napoleon, the Khans of Mongol, etc. *They are not the heroes for this writer,* though he admits them to be the bravest, skillful and intelligent muscular big-bullies, beyond belief when presented themselves on the **killing fields**. Unknowingly, they misused their extra brain capacities and thrived on the killing fields and *we have been trained to admire them for their capacity to kill.*

The real heroes for this writer appeared slowly and timidly only of late. All of them had the **intense curiosity about everything around them**. Some of them are Tycho Brahe, Kepler, Copernicus, Galileo, Newton, Faraday, James Clerk Maxwell, Einstein, Planck, (Abe Lincoln, Gandhi, Tolstoy) and many others of that type. They tuned their extra brain's capacity in the correct direction and no killing fields need be glorified in their names.

Notice that we can think of anything we choose without anyone noticing. Thinking always happens in the extra brain capacity region 3, illustration 13, which each one of us of us has.

Thinking is PURE hallucination that has not materialized into any muscular movements of the body.

Since thinking cannot be detected and involves no brain-ordered movements, by and large, it is free and could be harmless or harmful until passed on to the action side of the brain, regions 1 and 2.

All sorts of feelings "none needing muscular movements", such as memories, emotions, planning also lurk in the brain's extra capacity side. Most notable is the person's ego, born out of longstanding and continuously generated thinking—even if meant to be actionless. The ego does finally at some stage starts manifesting itself into some form of muscular movements of the homo-sapien, in the subtlest manners of speech, looks, head motions, and silence. Even a look by the homo-sapien has a few detectable microscopic muscle movements backed up by earlier thinking, a look into what one is thinking, or faking. A lot of ego's coating is always present in the individual's behavior. The chimp never expressed such emotion.

If the homo-sapien has detected self's ego and the conflicts it creates and he endeavors to become egoless, then there are no conflicts between his thinking (= hallucinating) in the brain's extra space of region 3 and resulting muscular actions from regions 1 and 2. *This is the most ideal functioning of all 3 regions working together.*

The extra brain space" activity slowly sets the habitual temperaments for a particular homo-sapien and gets the body going for the individual's detectable living patterns. In short, others get to know wat the individual does, and less importantly, what he says. Saying anything does involve some thinking at first, and it creates movements of "specifically ordered muscles" of the saying-body. Saying exits the body through one's mouth and saying is free for the individual and it could be *fairly harmless to extremely harmful*. No wonder advanced political systems rarely punish anyone for merely "saying anything" even if distasteful or harmful *in the context interpreted*. But, when a saying is understandable and interpretable, as heard by other homo-sapiens that do have varying rules of interpretations to refer to, the sayings may have legal consequences if it can be proven that others sprang into harmful action in one way or another as a result of the *purposeful* sayings to create social harm.

(a tune by the Fab-Four "think of what you are saying, you can get it wrong and still you think that it's alright"? Or this different tune by the same "you say yes, I say no, you say why? I say I don't know! Oh no!", just a fond memory for the writer)

There are about 8 billion people on our planet, and let us say about 50% of them are presently "doing" something and/or "saying / muttering" something. Others are simply thinking, = hallucinating or sleeping.

That is 4 billion people doing simple routine acts like thinking, which we cannot detect. Saying, which we can hear and interpret only. Doing things like eating, which we can observe needs no interpretation. "Thinking only" is pure hallucination using only the 3rd region of the brain. Saying, which does fairly agree with thinking even if it is contradictory to intentions in Region 3, uses all three regions.

Homo sapiens are the only ones that evolved and are accustomed to full violent reactions based on interpreting symbols of what is said or expressed as text. Interpreting is such a tricky subject that politics within large groups of homo-sapiens are accustomed to justified killings simply based on sayings with no overt intentions or preparation for any actions from other sides. It goes to prove how quickly homo-sapiens are tuned to perform acts of killing and have no tolerance for hearing what they do not like. But the universe outside you at large does not give a hoot about what your brain is thinking or saying and never demands actions from you, either.

The question is, how in the heck did all preferences the homo-sapien gravitated towards happens to be violence for multitudes of reasons, rather than a preference for peaceful accommodation, when the growing brain could have accommodated that as the better preference is not that mysterious? The extra capacity of the brain could have gone the better way accommodating the entire homo-sapien species, after it became apparent that the earth's resources that the homo-sapien desperately needs are scattered very non uniformly. The firmly embedded ego never let homo-sapiens develop resources in a cooperative way. Now that we have come to a stage when that needed principle is realized, erred political systems are scrambling hard to achieve better methods of co-operation.

There is a region on the earth where the stated a better choice has been *made in a more or less way*. It is the original Indian subcontinent. Created within the last 5000 years are *at least 3 major systems on living in peace*. All of them cater to **nonviolence as a core principle** and cooperative living and accommodation as the norm (Hinduism, Jainism, and Buddhism).

Compared to the chimp, which does not have region 3 of Illustration 13, the child can learn to load up his region three with truth-based teachings. If the truths are belief based the child is not encouraged to question the validity of anything, Fortunate is the child whose caretakers have evolved to encourage a child to question anything, prove an answer, and show various methods of finding evidence.

The real beginnings of science start approximately with Copernicus. Strange that how much in error was his own religion and its beliefs, since he must have realized they were hallucinated ideas with no verifications ever given. Such errors were being discovered more by those who were mentored to teach that very religion than by the disconnected homo-sapiens at large. Copernicus was one such person, a preacher timidly turned into a scientist. Boy-oh-boy, have we been screwed for so long by being forced to learn through religion, things and processes that never existed at all?

All the greats of ancient Mesopotamia, Persia, Greece, Rome, Egypt, and much neglected India, China, and others of the East all of them erred for eons when they relied on the advice from supernaturals for their major killing campaigns. So long to the Oracle of Delphi, the pseudo supernatural.

Once they were discovered, - the methods of science that is, you and this writer are irreversibly assured of better health, transportation, security and food supply. *No royalty ever enjoyed such modern luxury* that we commoners enjoy today. Even mere 100 years ago anesthesia, proper surgical tools, medicines, hospital and speedy well-equipped ambulances with good roads did not exist. Picture all the amputations and field side surgeries of the crippled without anesthetic, in all the killing fields between fighting groups, before medical science became advanced enough. Copernicus made us understand how the solar system goes about, but that may be knowledge that very few can use. Yet he set the systematic investigative technique for others for more useful subjects. Darwin unraveled, with a broad brushstroke, the mystery of *how anything living behaves*. He showed that which told us that we are all related as distant cousins. The discovery of the existence of the 3 billion rung DNA spiral (by Johann Friedrich Miescher), contained in every living cell, describes how we will stay related, distant cousins always. No living thing can be created *unless self-duplicating DNA is already available*.

The real heroes of science are many who rapidly show up from about the times of Copernicus. Here are *just a few* names: Copernicus (1473 – 1543), Kepler (1571 – 1630), Galileo (1564 – 1642), Newton (1642 – 1727), Faraday (1791 – 1867), James Clerk Maxwell (1831 – 1879), Planck (1848 – 1947), Einstein (1879 – 1955), etc., and so many, *many*, **many** others.

Several of the above, Darwin included, literally faced death threats for exposing what they knew to be true while fully knowing that *what others thought to be true* in their beliefs and faiths were in reality false. They, for reasons of fear and punishment, were shy or scared of publishing their findings. Today, how far have we come, and how quickly have we come so far because of those great scientists?!

Could you believe Copernicus agreed to publish his heliocentric solar system only on the certainty that his death was imminent? Could you believe Galileo could not convince anyone to look at the moon to prove that it is full of blemishes (craters)? He bravely annoyed the Pope to the extent that in his last few years, he was under house arrest.

All of them, not being individual islands in self, credited their mentors on whose shoulders, as Newton would say, they stood on.

Not included are non-scientific geniuses and great persons like Abe Lincoln (1809 – 1865), Tolstoy (1828 – 1910), Gandhi (1869 -1948), etc. Because they are of a different type. The theme of this write-up does not call for their talents. Frankly being a bit negative, if these latter three had lived longer, they just might have delayed scientific progress by a bit through their faith rhetoric, but would have done it absolutely innocently, not really knowing what science is all about.

Briefly stated here are their mentors: for Copernicus / Domenico Ferrara, for Kepler / Michael Maestelin, for Galileo / Guidobaldo del Monte, for Newton / Isaac Barrow, for Faraday / Humphry Davy, for James Clerk Maxwell / William Hopkins, for Max Planck / Helmholtz, for Albert Einstein / Max Talmey, and so on.

Credit is due from the writer to Richard Dawkins for glorifying Darwin (1809 – 1882) to be more than just a name in science but to be the greatest in the most forceful manner.

Further, learning more about Darwin through the BBC series and the ship Beagle definitely put Darwin's name among the foremost genius scientists (for the writer) of all times. Darwin clearly put forward on firm grounds how living things are related through hundreds of thousands of evolutionary steps and *natural selection,* which happens to be quite mean process, in homo-sapien outlook.

We all have slightly differing brain sizes but all have enough of the region 3 the extra capacity. Unless the extra capacity's utilization is mentored, we stay average or worse. Darwin was very fortunate in every way to use his brain's extra capacity to become a genius. He had the background of his family, relatives and others (such as Henslow) to keep his curiosity about nature at a high level *24/7.* The immensity of his curiosity got a start very early into the testing grounds of all over the earth when he signed up to sail with the Beagle for 5 years, with the annoying Tory Fitzroy as his captain.

Devoid of ego and replete with curiosity, these above scientists had found the proofs and evidence of the realities of life, living, material processes, and other things in the universe. It is extremely rare for parents to have the ability to mentor their child since parents are normally incapable of being objective about their children. Would you believe Darwin's father wanted Darwin to become a physician like him? When Darwin rebelled, he asked him to become a pastor! *Where is the logic in that switch*, but except for the constant encouragement to study and learn? Couldn't he see the intense curiosity in the kid about nature?

Charles Darwin's mentor was John Stevens Henslow, his professor. They both were intensely curious naturalists. After school hours they behaved more like partners in friendship through their walks into nature. It was Henslow who was slated to be the naturalist on the English ship Beagle that was to sail around and map S American continent, and then map the rest of the word into far west. Adding a naturalist to simultaneously collect specimens from the land and seas was an afterthought. You see, give credit to the English who were intensely curious about the world from a scientific point of view no doubt, *while having simultaneously deep mean intentions politically to plunder far off lands.*

Henslow could not go, and so he "strongly/unhesitatingly" recommended his student Darwin. Such is the power and benefit of a mentor's observation of capacities in another homo-sapien. Darwin was barely 22 when he went on the five-year voyage and almost immediately his mere natural curiosity of nature turned on the latent genius in him to look at everything through scientific reasoning. Everything he witnessed was new to him, including dust and sand that blew off of African coast and settled *on that side of the sail's masts.*

Darwin will be fondly remembered forever for being an early true scientist though he was not fully educated in that field. But the Beagle's captain, Fitzroy, a Tory, will only be remembered for interfering with Darwin's work till the day he died; *a great example about the stubbornness of one's ego* and false belief system impounded into a him from birth.

The evidence against Fitzroy's stubborn erroneous beliefs in god-etc. was being continuously presented for all the five years during Darwin's voyages. Again, such is the mutual hold of ego and stubbornness even while clear evidences were explained right in front in reach for Fitzroy to touch, smell, see and hear, and understand. Ripe and ready as Darwin's brain was for observation and absorption, with both those qualities growing exponentially, he became a changed homo-sapien because of this voyage and all the new worlds he witnessed and never stopped his investigations on the theory of evolution in life, to the day he died. Credit also goes to Alfred Russel Wallace, who almost contemporaneously went and studied the far eastern Asian islands in a similar way to Darwin.

Coincidentally, Darwin and Abe Lincoln are "exact" contemporaries to the date of birth, two greats but worlds apart in temperaments and situations of the given options to be progressive, and standards of living while growing up. Abe was born into abject poverty, but through sheer

THE KITH AND KIN OF HANUMAAN

determination and curiosity, he learned to read mostly by himself. We do not think he knew anything about evolution or had time to learn what Darwin was up to. It is a great saga of Abe's life as he is seeking his options in learning to read on own, his father is discouraging through butt-whipping to curb his curiosity in reading. On the contrary in apposition Darwin was extremely lucky to have understanding parents and other mentors around him all through his growth years. Wonder how many such-whipped kids for eons were thoroughly discouraged against their natural curiosity, let alone not being mentored into it!

Wonder how Abe would react to the knowledge that we, including America's slaves, are distant cousins as proved by Darwin, and that all of us descended from apes of Africa, while ironically slavery was still at a frenzy in both Americas, all around during their lives. Darwin saw plenty of cruel slavery in South America and openly abhorred it since he was a decent Englishman and they the English were on the verge of abolishing. Abe saw plenty of it in N America *and secretly abhorred it* since he was into politics and could not openly admit his liberal views fully. Abe probably could have never been able to afford to travel the world and meet Darwin, even if temperaments permitted. Tolstoy of noble stock, though not a full and exact contemporary, shares many common years of living in the same years with Abe and Darwin.

Having been part of some great wars in the post Napoleonic era of Europe, though is a great writer, he struggles to find peacefulness and real meaning in living a correct life. *He innocently reverts into more and more of the belief system* inclusive of **god-etc**., but to the definite purpose of complete non-violence in homo-sapien living. He had the right idea but wrong belief. Tolstoy knew about Abe's greatness and his accomplishments, but the writer wonders how both would react to Darwin, who knew the truths on evolution better than either of them. It appears Tolstoy, as he aged, became more religious with exceptional morals and ethics towards the less fortunate that were being subjugated under the Romanov kings.

Darwin, once he realized the true nature of evolution, finds everything supernatural, especially the notions in **god-etc.**, going out of him forever bit-by-bit. It seems Darwin would accompany his wife to church. With all the evidence and the greatest scientist at her shoulder, stubbornly she could never accept the evolution of homo-sapien from ape. Darwin would not attend church services with his wife but hung around outside the church waiting for her to come out. Another great example of stubbornness combined with ego in his wife refusing to see evidence, which could not be any closer to anyone.

These profound scientists, "observer-cum-experimenters-cum-thinkers," (note, thinking is relegated to the last spot) had to bear insults and serious threats from those early converts of holy-men clinging to their supernatural beliefs. The religious converts had the support of both types of big-bullies. By now *The big-bullies of the holy-man kind were not only wrong, but they were never correct for centuries.*

Let the writer ask, does any one of those must-know "*quitabs* (books, testaments)" start with some lines of this sort; "Being born is to learn foremost how to enjoy living in a proper responsible manner for your full life's term. Be curious about this universe and unravel all your brain so you can to understand it. You have the brains. Though the universe may not care about you a bit, you must care about it "a whole lot" all through your life. It will not spend any time understanding you, but you spend all your time understanding it and your fellow homo-sapiens".

Is there a religious book-*quitab* that glorifies enough to include in it the findings on (let alone explain) gravity, electromagnetics, elements, thermodynamics, etc.?

10,000 years ago, at the beginning of The Modern Evolutionary Era, our average brain was only just 1.7 cc smaller. i.e., instead of being 1400 cc, it was 1398.3 cc, 99.9%! *So, we did have the needed brains then* and much before too, to accomplish all that has been realized in the past few hundreds of years! *But we had been misusing our brains in the wrong direction already for tens of thousands of years.* Blame systems of faith and the super ego of all the types of big-bullies keeping us down in the dirt.

Look at anyone you admire or consider smart, intelligent, creative. **Such accolades will rarely be directed to that person's religiosity**. It will always be directed to his secular education.

No one is just born with a good brain and became great. They did have the brain, but then it must have been nurtured. A great example of modern days on mentorship, is Michael Phelps who had a super mentor to coach him with total support from Michael's mother.

Note: No one is leaving this earth and going anywhere to colonize for hundreds or thousands of years, no matter how smart we become with ever enlarging brains. The ultra materially rich big-bullies along with other cooperating big-bullies need to understand this and tone down their egos about space travel and wastage of resources and pollute the environment. So much better is to join hands with ordinary homo-sapiens and increase the disappearing habitable green regions on this earth. Please don't waste your riches on egotistical, wasteful plans.

Section 14: First set of Zigzag Migrations with Backtracking

The bipeds (say 7 million years ago) that turned into homo-*whatevers* (say 6 to 3 million years ago) must have moved about in "zigzag backtracking patterns," originally all across Africa not knowing where they were going. At some point, they entered the rest of the earth's reachable lands. (For clarity here, a biped is a chimp that walks on two all the time but clearly looks like a chimp, and a homo-*whatever* is a hominin / human looking advanced evolution stage of a biped.) The brain growth gene must have been present in the original bipeds *already.* It is estimated that, in a million years or two, the homo-whatevers could have traversed the whole of the African continent. The average size brain of homo-*whatevers,* even if groups were thousands of miles apart, should have been about 900 ccs 3 million years ago since today—a fairly large size.

The writer cannot help but assume that some genetic changes in bipeds happened in all of them when they were still the original small group. Hence when groups split into more groups, all migrated groups were subject to the same genetic changes. That is, same genetic mutations could have occurred in various biped groups even after they moved away from each other's proximity, but maybe at slightly at different rates.

This 900 cc being the average size, giving the homo-whatevers thinking capabilities, the direction and amount of thinking (read - hallucinating) could have varied widely between individuals and between groups as whole units. When groups bumped into each other as very distant cousins, sexual desires naturally must have been aroused, leading to conflicts **and killings**. (See illustrations 1, 2, 4, 5, and 6.)

The reader must keep a few facts in mind at all times: **1.** *that only homo- sapiens remained* by the beginning of The Evolutionary Modern Era, meaning homo-sapiens had reached all the far corners of earth's everywhere by the beginning of The Evolutionary Modern Era, which includes thousands of islands and spans over 22,000 miles of end-to-end distances. **2.** Further, all these homo-sapiens discovered *did have* some form of belief system in the supernatural that seemed to have a hold on their present lives and their imaginations of after-death lives.

The chimps, from whom the hominins emerged over 6 million years ago were already temperamentally cruel, having group against group brutal killings inclusive of occasional cannibalism. No hominin group, no matter how enlarged their brains or smarts were, had any inkling of what a scientific investigative method was *though they could have dwelled into it* even with a much lesser than full brain size. The water thinks the predominance of physical dominance and sexual desires prevented any such creativity. Most importantly, finally, a normal homo-*whatever* individual had his brain thoroughly trained to severely subjugate himself to the groups" muscular big-bullies; he thus developed a perpetual big-bully syndrome.

The radiating lines to thousands of miles by bipedal homo-whatevers, as shown in many illustrations by others, *do not make sense* without pointing to localized random zigzagging and backtracking for hundreds or thousands of years and then getting pushed out to new locations.

The localized zigzag patterns shown in illustrations 5 and 6, covering ultimately entire continents, may make more sense as to be the true nature of migration, until a few thousand years before The Evolutionary Modern Era 10,000 years ago. Migrations till then must have been at the whims of muscular big-bullies based on his desires for food, territories, and sex. Slavery and serfdom of modern times are good examples that point out that the subjugated do not think for themselves even if they have the capacity of which they are ignorant. Being pushed around to severe extreme limits only brings out the courage for Bastille day or October revolution.

Here are some history basics of the evolution of mammals in general before the ultimate specialized mammal, - **us**, got evolved: About say, 500 million years ago, large landmasses such as Europe, Americas, Siberia,

Asia and others joined to form a single landmass called **Gondwana** that had no ocean passages within it. A single ocean surrounded Gondwana. Most of the water of the world was already here on earth in the oceans and Gondwana had fresh water lakes, rivers, etc. Fairly large and complicated swimming predators in the seas were already well evolved from the billions of years of past. They obtained their oxygen through water. There were no creatures really to speak of anywhere on the lands of Gondwana. It did have rudimentary plants and trees evolving over the next 200 million years.

Some shallow water dwellers in the ocean with sturdy fins, and fairly midsize bodies crawled on their stiff fins onto the land for amphibious living (Tektaalik!) about 380 million years ago. This was the beginning of animal life on lands. That is, we all on land started as fish, Tektaalik descendants.

Tektaalik eventually evolved into hard crusted egg-laying reptiles that evolved to live permanently on land and not being amphibians anymore. The reptiles then turned into all sorts of dinosaur type creatures (still reptiles). These permanent land dwellers roamed all the interiors while Gondwana started to split up into continents that you know of today. Everyone knows about the roaming of dinosaurs (250 to 66 million years ago). For a good perspective, compare their ~180 million-plus years of living on Earth, by dinosaurs etc., and their types to our homo-sapien's puny existence of maybe less than 75,000 years as "us". All evolved creatures on land were originally egg-laying types, inherited from fish. You can *believe that a homo-sapien mama still carries a redundant egg* when pregnant! Until about 125 million years ago, no land animal on Gondwana evolved into live birth-giving "mammals," to bypass hard shelled egg-laying.

It is possible that about this time Gondwana was breaking into two sections (~ 180 million years ago): Western Gondwana containing Africa and South America. As a unit they separated from Eastern Gondwana, consisting of all the rest (North America, Europe, Asia, Australia, India, Antarctica). The final further breakup of Gondwana as we know into the continents of today, of all the earth's landmasses continued, perhaps, until 25 million years ago. The most significant breakup was Africa getting separated from South America, giving rise to the *wide* mid-Atlantic with a ridge making a continental divide at the Atlantic Ocean, all of it at the ocean bottom. This very wide oceanic gap between Africa and N America is what we call the Atlantic.

Then evolved *very small creatures,* many of them called mammals because they bore their offspring in their wombs for long periods of time until they were ready to be born. Because of the dominance of the humongous reptiles surrounding them, they remained small and lived in burrows. Gondwana, as it split up, had originally given many land accesses to all mammals and the larger creatures. Then, due to the well-known episode of a very large meteor striking the Yucatan region, all large creatures perished completely albeit over a few million years. Especially the predator types perished, about 66 million years ago leaving their **big bones as fossils on every continent.**

With ripe opportunities then, though the first evolved mammals were small shrew-sized creatures, they grew larger with no predators hunting them after the Yucatan incidence. Understand that all these various mammals are cousins—not necessarily 1st, 2nd, or may not be even the 1000th —but still are cousins. In fact, Tektaalik was their mama.

Gondwana broke up permanently into the continental landmasses and islands as we know today. With snow and ice accumulating in the polar regions due to repeated ice ages every tens of thousands of years, the ocean's water levels lowered significantly, giving all creatures (including homo-*whatevers,* - millions of years later) access to travel between Siberia to North America, South America, and Far East Asia to many lands and islands, including Australia and beyond. This travel was always on land since traveling on water did not get invented until we were late in The Evolutionary Modern Era devising boats. With hundreds of millions of years of our distant creature-cousins requiring to evolve, "us homo-sapiens" seem to have required only 6 million years to accommodate all the spectacular changes in us from our ancestor the chimp. The chimps of today, and probably back 6 million years ago too, are comfortable living within a radius of about 5 miles, as long as their own kind are around and they have enough food.

Give a few of these individual groups of chimps each a 25 x 25-mile region (equivalent to a large city with suburbia), and that would support many generations, perhaps from hundreds to thousands of years. They may have been pushed out into new regions every 500 years or so by stronger zigzagging biped groups moving in.

No group could cross water or run around at night. No biped family unit, as we know it, had formed yet, but no chimp is an island by itself, and hence each chimp must have remained loyal to some group under the wings of its big-bully.

The instinct of fighting to kill and eliminate other existing groups of its own type as a rule may not have developed yet, but this combination of a growing brain, opposable thumbs giving super dexterity, and running on two legs must have been in the works of creating elaborate changes in their confident living styles of the bipeds and future hominins.

No single group could have roamed all over Africa with the intention of dominating the entire continent by itself, but do not forget that only one type, **us**, remained all over the world by the beginning of The Evolutionary Modern Era. The instinct to dominate other groups could be a genetic trait that was developed early, and hence all groups, all over, may have developed similar instincts to dominate anything they faced, especially when faced with their own type.

It might have taken half a million to 1 million years for the bipeds to reach all of the far oceanic borders of Africa without any knowledge of their ancestors" origins. It is possible that, within this time period, some groups zigzag backtracked into the Levant region through Sinai and then beyond. Chances are the Sinai was not always an inhospitable desert.

Still, basically still looking like chimps, even with advanced evolutions in "legs," vocals, brain size, and the ability of making of better offensive-defensive tools using ever better opposable thumbs, they must have faced many other arboreal chimps *and primates* and bipeds similar to them, no matter where they went in Africa.

Once the sea coasts became an edge not to be crossed, descendants could have backtracked in any and every direction into the lands, not knowing that their bipedal ancestors must have lived in those regions for hundreds of thousands of years and also in the regions they are about to cross in the interior. See illustrations 2, 3, and 4 for how someone (with super homo-sapien powers bestowed) looking down from space on the entire African continent, more or less uniformly covered with early bipeds and homo-*whatevers*, would have seen **the constant kill-them-all skirmishes**. No other ground-living creature would give you that appearance of constant zigzag backtracking and frequently fighting as groups. The homo-whatevers, all over, were becoming naturally smarter in their own ways while traveling.

A chimp wanders about 2 x 2 miles in a day. Let us say, as a start, its bipedal cousin will walk 4 x 4 miles per day. It might do this with its group for its entire lifetime of 30 or so years unless pushed out by other big-bullies or food shortages. It is expected, though, to stick to its group, with no courage to go off by itself.

Soooooo, say for a few hundred years, its descendants may be comfortable within 400 squares miles, i.e., 20 x 20.

For a thousand years, they may hang around in an area of 3,000 square miles (about 55 x 55 miles square).

Africa is 11.7 million square miles. Let us assume the occupiable area for chimps is less, about 6 million square miles.

Soooooo… (6,000,000 sq miles /3,000 sq miles) x 1,000 years = 2,000,000 years, time taken to walk all over Africa.

This means that if the African continent had no land bridges to the rest of the world, the bipedal homo-whatevers would cover all of Africa in 2 million years—theoretically.

But since they could go out via the Sinai passage, and the groups could explore the rest of the world on two legs, such an exit could have happened in the first million years of wanderings. No group would know, from one 50 years to the next fifty years, where they would end up, and all the roaming would be zigzag, back and forth, random, with innocently retracing old paths. The wanderers might stick, initially, to amiable climatic conditions to avoid extremes.

New generations would come across other new or old generations after 500, 10,000, 100,000, or 500,000 years, not knowing they were all cousins mating with cousins from the distant past. Bipedal homo-whatevers that trekked deep into Asia, Russia, Europe, or South Africa might never backtrack again into the initial African regions, not by any plan of course. Instead, they may encounter aggressive newcomers of their own type all the time who have been advancing, and pushed themselves farther and farther far away.

So far, all the brain growth must have been focused on developing better killing tools for hunting or defending against enemies of any creature types, like wolves, hyenas, etc., while the muscular big-bully's task was to maintain his superiority in all respects of encounters while protecting what is his.

No religious individual or religious zeal or concept of religion had entered into the manners of the living of homo-*whatevers* **yet**.

Working backwards in time from today, it appears that supernatural religious fervor could have been initiated and progressed rapidly from somewhere in the regions of Sinai, Anatolia, Caucasus, or Levant etc. This is just a guess based on the recorded history of today and research into about 1000 years before The Evolutionary Modern Era.

The ideas of supernaturalness could have started anywhere, and spread around. Based on supernatural beliefs and the zeal to dominate others in new beliefs is different than dominance through muscular big-bulliness. (It is so much more fun, entertaining, creative, to proselytize when some never known ideas of **god-etc.** are hallucinated and explained to so many individuals *that need to be converted*.) Let us imagine that the religious fervor (supernatural of course) for the very first time could have started somewhere in China or India and then backtracked into the Caucasus or Levant regions to further blossom there, but this does not appear to be the case based on the research *by westerners* if their research is to be accepted as unbiased. No insurmountable physical barricade of the size of the Himalayas and Hindu Kush exists as an impediment for zigzagging and backtracking groups in the Levant and near about regions. The movements into clinging on to newly acquired supernatural belief does not look like it happened ½ or 1 million years ago but 10 to 5 thousand years ago, *before* The Evolutionary Modern Era of 10,000 years. Why so late when the average brain size was ripe to explode at *any time since tens of thousands of years ago* is not necessarily a mystery when one looks at the tight control of the big-bullies. Again, look at the slaves and serfs, how long they remained so without ever questioning.

If one would like to contend that the earliest supernatural beliefs started well before the years stated above, then the writer counterargues that the existence of several more independent *advanced centers of religiosity should be possible*. There could be a possibility that initial religiosity started with the penultimate species (Neanderthalensis?) instead of homo-sapiens! No such widely separated multi-religiosity locations appear in research. Everything points to N E Africa.

Even if the religiosity concept started with a penultimate species to homo-sapiens, homo-sapiens could have absorbed it fully and eagerly and spread it in every direction possible, with unbelievable zeal (- better follow our ways or else!), killing away all other homo-*whatever* species that did not get along with the new ideology. This type of religious zeal is believable because such things of pressures happened in the writer's own life time.

Why is this strong assumption by the writer on homo-sapiens with religious fervor of conversion—or-else-kill-them-all attitude until the end? *Because we found only homo-sapiens existing after we became able enough to travel all over the world* – not a single hominin of earlier species was encountered, *which means we killed all others*;

- and further, even the farthest reaches of the world had some form of god-etc. belief systems showing that the initial fervor of zeal of initial religiosity did get carried to far off lands,

- and the farther we went into Siberia, the Americas, Germanic lands, and into the large and small down-under lands and islands, and even into the Germanic regions of Europe the more ancient and rudimentary the religious practices were being practiced, which indicates that they the homo-sapiens of these regions were recipients of the very original religious belief systems.

Remember that once homo-sapien religiosity had gotten established at the earliest rudimentary level, and as it spread farther out due to zealots, any backtracking for catching up with further sophistications happenings in the belief systems would not have reached all corners that were too much farther out and distant. This also fairly proves that religiosity started through clever thinking and deep emotions rather than truly experiencing the presence of a god or a creator. **Such an experience is impossible any way except through hallucination and so, no such thing as god ever existed.**

Also, all belief systems, no matter how primitive or sophisticated, were supernatural-based, confirming that they all had a common ancestral beginner region at some indefinite location. The writer is ready to accept this location to be N E Africa to the Levant axis regions rather than some location on the Indian subcontinent or China. Definitely birth of religion did not happen in the extremely far off regions and back tracked into Africa.

It must be firmly understood that there is no implication of which system is better or where it is better or superior—none whatsoever. Since all were based on supernatural, *they were all fundamentally false anyway no matter however superior sounding*. Since, at core, all religions are based on supernatural beliefs, they are all false to begin with, no matter how deeply charismatic preachers they had. But they had the ability to fool everybody. The fear of afterlife and the allure to ritual must have been, and still are, deeply attractive. Familiarity in religions breeds deep respect and love, because it addresses one's fears of death and after, albeit falsely. Please firmly note that this writer fully rejects all supernatural beliefs in favor of human, natural, humanistic, homo-sapien-based, pacifistic systems.

It is highly unlikely that the **god-etc.** systems originated in several locations independently, hundreds or thousands of miles apart, somewhat simultaneously or at various timings, and all of them propagated radially from their multiple central regions, and then they all merged into some central system. With no scientific tools available as we have today, mass communication before The Evolutionary Modern Era or until recently was not possible.

Zigzagging, backtracking, brain growth, increased intelligence leading to rigid one male to one female relationships, accentuated with newly evolved religiosity – *all these factors must have developed more or less concurrently* in various groups. The above attitudes also resulted in continued zest for killing / elimination of inferior groups. All the while extensive physical sexuality changes were happening to the homo-*whatever* body. The sexuality changes in us in relation to chimps were extensive and multi-faceted, especially to the homo-*whatever* female. A sexually active homo-*whatever* could be sexually active throughout the year for extended number of decades, especially the male.

If the homo-sapiens of 10,000 years ago to now, that is in The Evolutionary Modern Era, had not developed superior metal tools, - and permanency in social communication through written records of oral utterings, and travel over large bodies of water using newly developed floating vessels, if these would not have happened; we homo-sapiens of today would have stayed isolated for much longer periods of time and would not have known each other's ways of living until much later. The homo-whatever continued developing lethal weapons well beyond as needed for hunting gathering. He used them to fight and kill his own types!

On the contrary, with the increasing size of the brain, but for the wrong directions taken by homo-sapien's egos and the ever present big-bullies (of all types), we could have arrived at the general prosperity as enjoyed today much earlier, because our brains at about only 3 ccs less than 1400 ccs, were large enough for all the needed intelligence even 5k to 10k years ago before the start of The Evolutionary Modern Era. With the continued growth of the brain, there should probably be a newer species of us, say, in about 150 thousand to 250 thousand years from now.

What physical changes will it manifest in us *then*? What physical changes in sexual behavior will it instill in us? Will we of today will become the new Neanderthals of the new species then?

Though we have much control over the use of our intellect, we may not have any control over the mutations of our DNA. No matter how deep our itch is to colonize, it is highly unlikely that we will ever find a suitable place in space or our abilities will be advanced enough in space travel to go far enough and colonize some distant planet.

Assuredly, thousands of years from now, we will not have the unique variations in our looks we have today,

- like Europeans and their variations,
- like Asians and their variations,
- like Semites and their variations,

because we would have intermingled thoroughly, soon enough by then.

The earth never remained or remains materially homogeneous throughout. The 100 or so elements and their compounds are plenty enough but are dispersed non-uniformly all over earth, water supply varies widely in various regions, and soil conditions have enormous differences. From hot, dry deserts to super fertile arable fields elsewhere is the norm. Of course, though the earth can make many compounds, and we can make any element *artificially,* the earth can never make any element naturally. Only stars can do that. Radioactive elements that breakdown naturally and form two elements are an exception but that is not making elements.

Regions of extreme climate will always need supplies from regions with favorable climate. Status quo may be okay, but in a few hundred years from now, global cooperation in natural sciences may become the undisputed needed rule to be followed. This necessitates toning down egos by everyone and cooperating in all useful sciences should become a routine. By helping develop unproductive lands into becoming productive regions, mass migrations (a very displeasing subject) into richer lands could be curtailed.

After continuous zigzagging and backtracking for almost 6 million years, the final zeal to go over all the lands must have happened about 5,000 to 10,000 years before The Evolutionary Modern Era.

This is when the writer thinks:

- The concept of religion started,
- The zealous spread of religion took place (**),
- The killing or enslaving of inferiors happened everywhere,
- The variation in looks between distant tribes got initiated,
- The sexual bodies of females changed fully to that of today,

- The extended sexual appetite periods for homo-sapiens got established,

- The various oral languages with immense sound differences got established.

(**) Unlike what could take place a mere 2,600 years ago, when hordes of well-equipped homo-sapiens could travel hundreds to a thousand miles or more using horses, chariots, ocean-going vessels, etc., the homo-whatevers of the past traveled on foot—that too only during the day and only on land.

Section 15: The Change of Physique, Chimp to Homo-Sapien

While most mammals, being our near ancestors, behave with an alpha male big-bully dominating his harem and his territory, chimps are polyandrous Male chimps of today have sex with any willing female chimp based on desires or the need to relieve some (mental) stress. Female chimps will, in a similar fashion, have sex with any male that notices their pink butts, an indication of ovulating. Chimps are today, and must have been 6 million years ago too, polyandrous.

So, it seems any female chimp (of today) may be carrying the sperm of several male chimps at any given small period of time. It can be said she may be gang-raped willingly and can say that child is hers but does not know who the father is.

We will assume, for lack of other evidence, the chimp social behavior was about the same 6 million years ago as it is today, - absolutely abhorrent based on our homo-sapien standards.

Soooooo, for us who evolved out of those chimps (and evolved we did!), we have thankfully reversed a few horrible trends of those immoral chimps.

First of all, we gravitated into the one big-bully-per-one-group system. The one with the biggest muscles has taken over, having harems like the other primates (silverback gorilla?). The one with the biggest chest-bashing biceps and triceps controls his private harem. A bit of a mean system it may be, but it may be a better system than the rampant immorality of chimps.

When, where, why and how did our behavior pattern get forced to conform to the system of one homo-sapien female to be with only one dedicated male homo-sapien, tied up for life through the artificially fabricated system called marriage—the writer is not sure.

Since just about all homo-sapien cultures in some form, agree to some rules between homo-sapien male-female intimacy, such rules must have been initiated many thousands of years ago, probably in the regions northeast and northwest of the Sinai region of Africa. Whether such rules had existed before The Evolutionary Modern Era of 10,000 years is not known. Even in The Evolutionary Modern Era of the last 10,000 years, it is clear that the muscular big-bullies dominated and maintained multiple harems in close quarters with them. The big-bully always got all the sex he wanted first, and many times, exclusively.

Monogamous relationships are uncommon outside of some birds, where some seem to stay coupled for life with each other as a natural course. It would be interesting to know if that rule is based on their DNA, and *did we inherit those bird brains?* The rules for monogamous birds are nature-enforced, whereas for homo-sapiens, the rules are political, moral, religious, and law-enforced. It may be possible that the monogamous relationship was introduced by the newly emerged bully-pulpit holy-man big-bully as a prerequisite to enter heaven which also is invented by him. The homo-whatevers are the only ones that can use their opposed thumbs and have foreplay with each other. Other creatures (primate exceptions) cannot even touch their genitals with their limbs.

Nothing surprises this writer when sex is the subject for home-sapiens: it is least talked about, most looked at, *and constantly on the minds of homo-sapien males.*

Look at the growing, permanently projecting homo-whatever female breasts once a female passes puberty. Not so for chimps. The requirement by various cultures to cover them up almost at-least 80% because of the 2% real-estate of the nipples or to cover over 100% in some very conservative cultures, is routine. Still even in the most conservative cultures the females have a way of attracting the attention of the males to their breasts even if 100% covered. The females are constantly staring at their own breasts while pretending to adjusting the garments around them.

When did that permanency of full breasts start as we evolved from the chimps? With homo-sapien female life cycles, breasts are 30% of the time for milk production and the rest 70% for the male's desire to squeeze and suck. No two ways about it; sexuality on breasts dominates breast feeding in homo-sapiens 70 to 30, totally unlike chimps.

About a female chimp's breasts? The male chimp seems to be *least bit "nosy"* about them. He wants his 10 seconds of 7 or so clean shots of **IT** at each encounter into the vagina and he is satisfied. About female Homo sapiens" breasts? The writer thinks male Homo sapiens can't stop looking at them and there must be more brain space assigned and consumed for delicate eyeball movements by both sexes in this regard.

Let us consider the sexual position changes when comparing homo-whatevers to chimps.

Please look at illustrations 11 and 12 as you read this area. One of the most intriguing changes in sexual positioning that happened to the female homo-sapien is when her vaginal tract rotated to become vertical for *may be* through hundred generations or so. This of course is a theorization of an intermediate stage in rotation from rear pink butt region to the frontal neutral color position of today.

The order of the three female openings (in homo-sapiens or chimpanzees, or mammals in general) is as follows: anus, vaginal opening, and finally the urethral opening. The anus is the farthest from the belly, located between the buttocks. In chimpanzees, the anus is positioned much higher, right under the tail, and chimps engage in mating from the rear—back of the female, penetrated by the front of the male. When a female chimp is ovulating, the glands in her buttocks become extremely swollen and red. Our females have lost this characteristic; when did that occur this writer wonders?

The arrangement of these openings (see illustration 11, 12) has shifted rotationally, approximately 45 to 50 degrees, from the back towards the belly button into the crotch area. No wonder the homo-sapien female has to swing wide and open her thighs during doing of **IT**!

The pink characteristics in the buttocks area have completely disappeared. Since all evolutionary changes are very slow, how long did this rotation and color disappearance take place, and how did it happen? Was it coordinated with other changes in the female, such as the permanent enlargement of breasts? Was the duration of these changes 10,000 years or what, averaging about 0.005 degrees rotation each year?

Which geographical region did this breast enlargement change start taking place and what time during the 6m years?

For the male, not much positional change of the male organ, but the anus did rotate down just as it did for the female.

Why are the testes of a male homo-sapien hanging out and down like that?

An explanation given is that the sperm needs a few degrees cooler surroundings than the 98.6°F of the body. The writer's theory is that they must be for the female's homo-sapiens to stare at, and also to push, pull and squeeze. The two degrees cooler requirement is surely baah-humbug. Pure hogwash, the writer says.

They hang out so that the female homo-sapien has something of the male to grab onto with opposed thumbs and play with during foreplay. You insist on better explanation because you argue that they have been out there hanging millions of years before homo-sapiens, *for all mammals?* Now, now, now…. **you are for forcing this writer** to explain the real reason why those gonads are hanging out there like yoyos….

The real point of the testes hanging out is that the females love the *bang-bang,* **bang-bang***,* **banging of the gonads** *against their vulva* during the impassioned actions of **IT**. Can you imagine a bison bull, a Kodiak bear, and a wolf walking around in freezing temperatures or lying in the snow, to nap, naturally exposing their testicles to those temperatures? The arguments of 3 deg. cooler now should change to 60 deg cooler. The temperatures are close to freezing the testicles! Soooooo, their balls have nothing to do with needing couple degrees of colder temperatures!

Regarding giving up its body hair, it must have been initiated early by the bipeds, since all the migrated bipeds in far off lands also inherited the mutation to shed hair off very early. It is difficult to imagine bipeds roaming into far-off distances and each group separately developing the trait of shedding hair. It also explains why bipeds moving into colder regions have no body hair because their ancestors already shed it when evolving in Africa and nearby.

The change of skin color must have happened only after the homo-whatevers reached their far-off locations. It appears to be a latitude-based environmental influence.

The changes in the coloring of hair and eyes may also be latitude-based, but all the variations and the retainment of head and facial hair pose enigmas. The distinction of hair growth patterns between males and female homo-sapiens is also difficult to explain since no such distinction seems to appear in chimps.

A lot of things between us and the chimps are distinctly different. The writer is not attempting to be a perfect anatomist.

Consider:

- Head
- Brain size growth
- Eyebrows

- Nose, protruding
- Mouth, face, lips
- Front limbs, shoulders, and hands
- Opposed thumbs and fingers, their extra ordinary development
- Exposed chest and organs" side in upright positioning
- Elimination of the tail
- Teeth
- shortened canines
- Vocals, the most extra ordinarily developed feature
- Butts
- Breasts
- Sexual traits
- Sexual positions, face to face
- Manipulation of sexual areas by lips and palms
- Sexual periods, lifelong sexuality
- Menopause
- Face

- Much flatter, many changes in looks and skin pigmentation
- Nose protruding
- No more pink butts
- Shift in sexual activity from back to front
- Shortened canine teeth
- Increased foreplay with palms and lips
- Sex with a female, whether she is ovulating and ready or not
- Covering sexually potent areas with clothes to avoid embarrassment!

The changes are so many and so varied, and yet so uniform in all existing homo-sapiens everywhere, that the writer is again forced to reiterate the following:

Rampant killing of inferior groups by superior groups appearing after zigzagging and backtracking must have gone on relentlessly, especially with the added modern zeal of religious beliefs initiated about 5,000 to 10,000 years ago before The Evolutionary Modern Era. The very first location for religious zeal is possibly in the regions already mentioned; - near Northeast Africa, the Levant, and the Caucasus regions. The migrating homo-sapiens reached their far-off destinations of Europe, Asia-China-

Mongolia, Asia-India-Far East, and finally the Americas and Down-Under lands with the new zeal motivating them. And since only homo-sapiens remained after victories in killings, all the physicality in us is accordingly so. Other hominins may have had other type of physical changes but we will never know.

One factor that the bigger brain did not tackle was the ever-growing influence of the new feelings of ego in each as individuals because the region 3 accommodated and nurtured it. Chimps don't seem to have any ego.

Complex group trust and distrust have evolved among us homo-sapiens. Follow whichever wisdom path you may by any wise-man, you will still be mistrusted simply for your looks, language, and demeanor, a strange development indeed.

People of a certain religion will instinctively gravitate to others of their own religion, in addition to race, ethnicity, or language type, even without knowing any other particulars, and they will ignore others due to distrust. This becomes a two-way street. Outside the religious meeting place, racial and ethnic prejudices surface, and separation occurs. Inside the religious space groupism gives security.

Gandhi wanted to accept the religion of the white male homo-sapien in India and Africa, and he was denied, simply based on race! One less Anglo here.

The Turks would not trust their Arab counterparts and hence stole children of any other ethnicity from their conquered territories and trained them to be trustworthy Turkish soldiers. The children of different ethnicity, race, and religion (0 to 6 years old) were trained to be loyal soldiers, and many of them took on continued leadership roles as Turkish. Such is the power of 0 to 6-year indoctrination. One can see, since belief system originates through homo-sapien thinking with no connection to the outside universe, it creates untold misery and killing fields while touting to be all encompassing for a homo-sapien's living!

You, the reader, must get accustomed to thinking in chunks of 2k or 3k years till at least the 10k years of past from today, and then learn mentally to jump by 10 to 20k years till about 50k, when homo-sapiens may have begun changing in their physical looks in relation to the world's far off regions.

It is very difficult to destroy bones (except by heat and fire), and they are rarely consumed as food by any other creature. Hence, bone fragments of most animals that lived all over should be around somewhere unless pulverized into extremely small sand-sized grains geologic factors. The same will be true for millions of hominins that lived the past 6 m years.

We homo-sapiens are the only ones who seem to group ourselves not just by species but by *SO MANY* other categories like tribe, religion, ethnicity, skin color, etc. Our group trust is a lot more complicated and is only partially instinctive.

With which homo-*whatever* did these primordial sounds of hominin start turning into intelligible words? Did all groups thousands of miles apart start developing their vocal cords at the same time, making word utterances? Again, "kill them all and only us to remain might give the final answer". It is much easier to invent a noun because it simply represents an object but it is much harder to develop a new verb and all its varying uses. Hence, the very process of developing spoken words into sentences must have fired the hallucination / imagination of the wiser homo-sapien.

The extra capacity of the brain is undoubtedly passed on to the child, but mentoring to use its capacity to think and imagine takes special effort by the caretakers (parents), and this may not be easily available or understood both by the parents themselves and their offspring.

Considering the female body, homo-sapiens have permanently modified their nipple regions into distinctly enlarged breasts with sexual overtones, whether they remain milk-bearing or not. They have become two additional sexual pleasure objects for the opposed thumbs and modified mouths. Animals do not have any such extra-feature usage.

Section 16: The Forever Two-Bag Baggage

No parent at their own young age of becoming a parent is mature or courageous enough to admit that they are permanently introducing false belief systems into their offspring that is just to be born, through tradition. One may remember that their R-Bags are overflowing with materials with evidence against doing such a thing, and yet they go seeking into their L-Bags. Conformity is a heavy weight that almost all of us carry.

When you came out of your mother's birth canal, imagine that you came out permanently attached with two empty bags very lightweight even for an infant and invisible

Even you are unaware of the bags" existence, one on your left side L-bag, the other on your right side, R-bag.

No one, including you, can see or feel them, but imagine that they will be there for the rest of your life.

One can erase the memories of the past but cannot erase the past itself. So, you and others may occasionally know what kind of "gist and other" goes into those bags as you grow old but really cannot empty them. They will contain all the gist that comes into your life.

This stuff will weigh the bags. You will feel the weighing down, tug, and pokes, constantly stirring your emotions, conflicts, and your living, but you will know these from the essence of the stuff in the bags, but will not know about the bags themselves.

You may intensely love and enjoy or may not love the all the experiences stuffed in the bags forever, and often the only solution is to remove the bothersome stuff in the bags from your memory, but not from the bags!

Some long-lost forgotten weighty contents will be stirred every so often as reminders for your pleasure and pain, by yourself and others, often bringing tears to your eyes.

You may have never met some of the people mentioned below, but they have/had access to your bags" contents—one or both the bags.

Just after the instance of your birth, several people held you constantly in rotation, with tender hugs, and often those upgraded to cheek-to-cheek contact and kisses with unintelligible tender doting words. Many of these adults may still be around you but you don't know them anymore. Some others you will never see again.

They start filling one of the bags with very soft little items called dolls and, supposedly, and also with important songs and humming.

Let us call this bag the L-bag that is getting filled up from the instance of your birth. Many of the homo-sapiens that surrounded you *then* and a few more times may never come back to visit you.

This kind of disappearance, of those who were allowed to be close to you when you were out in this world barely an hour, then days and months old, will happen.

Soon you will have totally unexpected new and unusual experiences filling your L-bag, *and you have no control of them.* So far, your experience has only been to get hungry, cry, get a nipple "of some sort" shoved to your lips, suck it up, and then go back to sleep.

Based on your caretakers (=parents) liking some authorized adults will very lovingly dip your whole body into "supposedly holy waters" while chanting strange words, making you temporarily uncomfortable. More such gist into the L-bag. You probably won't like it and start crying, for sure.

But immediate extra-affectionate hugs and kisses will follow and you are delighted. You are learning how the combination of total discomfort and intense love going together feels like—sort of sour and sweet in that order. "They" are in control, and you have no choice but let out your screams, *to their delight of course.* You will hear so much laughter, talking, clapping, and partying that you may even get to know what it is to be proud of the stuff filling your L-bag. The gist of everything happening including the sounds, songs, cheers *of others* are going into your L-bag. In a different case, a different type of adult will subject you to a little pain (only if you are a boy), tearing off forever some thin skin from your body as if to say, "you don't need that anymore ever". "They" have been doing it for thousands of years, *"and so it should be done now too,* to you"! No one in that partying group ever thinks of asking "do we still have to go through this nowadays?"

They" are in control, and you have no choice but let out your screams, to their delight of course.

Plenty of hugs and kisses follow while you are being bandaged for any bleeding. Your L-bag is stuffed up with different experiences this time.

As pointed out, this treatment is for the boy only, "so that supposedly he will have fewer problems" in the future, of which they are so certain!? Nonsense, they do it because *they want to do that first unneeded surgery*, and once you grow even you will probably back up that such a thing must be done. Mind you all this into L-bag only, and no attentions to the R-bag yet.

These procedures are done when you are still an infant and in no position to know or understand. But as you grow you will love all those things and more.

If they delay filling the L-Bag with their choices, the adults are too afraid that you may say vehemently "no" later. You have no fears yet, but they have so many concerns already what you should be, should become, and how should live.

Get this! In some groups, the infant girl's genitals are mutilated! Why? Because "she may get herself and others into trouble" when she grows up. Trust the writer, the adults will do a lot of such things to make their lives a bit easier as the child grows up into puberty. Hypocrites!

Soooooo, More stuff has gone into the L-Bag.

Many others make infants go through some other "ancient" procedures. Maybe there were good reasons once upon a time; *but today*? Do these adults ever really shut their pride and ego and really think about stuffing the L-Bag?

For instance, today, we can immediately correct any deformed limbs of the new born body, transplant malfunctioning organs, and if needed keep the infant for many days and weeks in the hospital for various corrective measures, and these other guys are focusing on mutilating the genitals of little boys and girls, and subjecting them to "crappy stuff"? Confession time, even the writer succumbed to the pressure coming from the doctors in relation to his own children. Dumb and baah-humbug. In today's living? we belong to so many "baaah-humbugs." Because our caretakers descended from *so many* baah-humbug generations! All these procedures were conceived in one's brain's 3rd region eons ago and slowly got added on to the supernatural beliefs of religions. We find and do so many good things through science, but those humbug religion-driven homo-sapiens will have nothing of it, especially when they can control what goes into the L-Bag and manipulate you with love and protection. Actually, they are secretly afraid what you might become if they do not go through all the baah-humbug procedures *of their liking* and stuffing your L-bag appropriately.

Incidentally, they always have a big cooked-up party as a follow-up, but you are allowed to sleep through it all. It's parties for you as the reason and you have no capacity to be in them.

All in all, as you rack up, days, months and years, you are becoming conscious of stuff going into your L-Bag, and as the times go by you really enjoy all the attention you get for cooperating. *You get the feeling of belonging, - the most important security for a homo-sapien,* and nothing can top that feeling of other stuff going into your L-Bag.

Lose a tooth or two, and some mysterious fairy puts money under your pillow.

You try to keep awake all night because some ho-ho-ho-hailing bearded guy is supposed to come when the clock strikes 12 in the night and leave for you an unbelievable number of presents.

Occasionally, when you feel sad for no reason, dad shows up from work with the best-looking horse—a horse that has a horn on it. You saw that so-called unicorn with your schoolmate, and she said, "You don't have one yet?" Your L-bag is missing a horned horse? That is all you needed to be depressed.

All these wonderful things and events start filling your L-Bag, and you are always on top of the world with its related "party atmosphere "and have *regular visits* to the so-called "church or temple or mandhir or some such other equivalent established holy-structure".

You even find the "very very important" leaflets about your faith (that is now and forever), lyrics, and even whole books and special symbolized beaded necklaces filling your L-Bag. With each one a party follows, *of course*, and you turn out to be such a party goer for such parties! It's all about you! Are these all important and harmless things in your L-Bag? (if you get the courage to reflect someday, you will find they are neither)

They grow hooks and sharp edges as you grow and those become chinks that tend to cling to you, only because you got them with their permanency when you could barely walk or talk, let alone question, and now you are helpless to get rid of the truly unnecessary items. So on and so forth, you will be babied so much with all the related rituals that you start enjoying all these with the attention on you they carry. *You are constantly (secretly encouraged to be) in the company of others that have similar L-Bags.* Some children become so adept at knowing the prose and poetry set out in the L-Bag so well that they can repeat it by heart fully even before they are six. By George, he's got it! The whole of the L-Bag is forming your personality for the future. You might even be chosen to appear on "Country **XXX** got Talent".

Your lips, cheeks, tongue, and arms have been making the cutest sounds by saying the things from your L-Bag, to the absolute delight of your caretakers.

(If you turned out to be a virtuoso in music like Mozart, you would have regular full-blown concerts of your own.)

It is an unbelievable pleasure for others to hear the child uttering flawlessly "**the entire book**, the qitaab, the pusthak."

You learn to respectfully reject contents in others" L-Bags if they do not match what is in your L-Bag. No need to be embarrassed because this is acceptable and expected for all with L-Bags of varying types.

Just 6 years of bag filling already determines your grave marker or its equivalent, though you may live 94 years more!

And then, *all of a sudden*, the importance of filling the L-Bag stops, normally at age 6! The gist of the L-Bag, to the delight of your caretakers, are firmed up in your whole being's personality, and it is not needed to focus on it anymore. (time to let all caring adults surrounding you to become hypocrites of sort almost instantly).

Nothing of any significance has gone into your R-Bag so far! It's been about 6 years so far, but things are about to change.

At about age 6, you start going to an accredited school for about the next 12 years until you are 18, and nowadays the schooling rarely ends there. It is followed up by normal 4 year college, 2 year graduate college and may be a PhD. *No one in any one of these schools will teach you anything that needs to go in the L-bag.*

In an unrealized manner, you start meeting kids of your age of all types carrying varieties of L-Bags based on what they have gone through for the last 6 years. But, you are not allowed to peek into their L-Bags. No, no, noooo. It is bad manners for you, but it is not so for your caring adults to peek and question *what is in the L-bags of your exciting new friends*. Your caretakers may notice that some "liberal caretakers" of your friends have already let their kids to start filling their R-bags. "Look ma, my friend here already knows that water is made with oxygen and hydrogen and, *that the sun does not rise and set* but simply shows up in east and disappears in west, as the earth rotates around itself. His uncle gave him a large globe for his birthday. He already knows what a latitude is."

Many follow the rule of not enquiring into a different type of L-Bag for their entire life, with no curiosity of that sort ever to know what sorts of junk resides in all sorts of L-Bags including the reader's and the writer's own.

Any curiosity only develops conflicts regarding the better-ness and correct-ness of what each has in their L-Bags. You can be sure your adults have enough of those conflicts already.

The differences in L-Bags do not give one the feeling of being different but the feeling of strangeness. "How and why can they believe in that and those things?"

It does not occur to either that both could have incorrect and false stuff *because they are supernatural beliefs* in L-Bags.

One may definitely have the deep-down silent proud impression that his L-Bag's contents are better and superior, against what is in someone else's L-Bag if different and "so-strange". They have been taught to think so and never question that their care takers are right.

With the start of (secular) school for all ~ 6 year-olds, it is time to start filling R-Bags with new type of gist of what is being taught at school about, nature, science, and math. *Mind you! Those who have been filling your L-Bags suddenly convert themselves to insisting that "this school stuff" is extremely important and you better start paying attention to the teachers.* No equivalence to this hypocrisy exists. From here onwards, you are encouraged to ask, peek, compare, and question anyone's **R-Bag stuff** and how to understand whatever is going in it.

The teacher's R-Bag is so full of stuff that you can barely make out that he may have her own L-Bag and he takes extra precautions to be sure that his L-bag stuff never comes out for any kid to identify it and.

He dares not reach out, correctly so, into his own L-Bag while teaching.

It is curious and strange that the same caretakers who meticulously cared about your L-Bag are eager to see that someone called a "teacher" fills your and others" R-Bags with identical stuff and so that you don't get left out. It is a bizarre change in attitudes for everyone.

You never ever really doubt or grasp this sudden switch in attitudes of your caretaker adults *to trust these teachers* to fill your R-bag with all sort of new stuff, which by the way is the same all over the world with all teachers. Everyone everywhere learns the same that O2 and H combine to make the same type of water each and every time. In fact, you are encouraged to do extra stuff beyond the what the teacher teaches, and you yourself feel like doing all the extra stuff, and get way ahead in your everyday classes, *because all of it so exciting*. Some kids work so hard at their smarts being encouraged for the first time that they finish their 12 years of schooling in 8 or less (remember Mozart! And his genius).

Every day these caretaker adults insist that you (read – all of you children regardless of your L-Bags) read, memorize, write, recite, and do your homework on whatever is going into your R-Bag.

"Did you do your homework? Let me see," they pressure you in that manner constantly every day. Nothing like that ever took place with your L-bag stuff! There never was any homework then!

Hmmmmm…the L-Bag never really had any homework. All you had to do was more or less agree to the gist in there.

You never really had to keep up with the L-Bag stuff. Your caretakers kept that up on your behalf.

Don't understand something that went into your R-Bag today? Why was that hard to understand? You mean, from here onwards, I have to start understanding all that goes in there so that I don't fall behind and "flunk"? This truth is so taxing on so many. The L-Bag was a privilege to stay free and frolicking in the club of your kind. For what goes into your R-Bag, you have to earn every bit of credit and 20 other kids around you every day are watching! Hmmmmmm…never had to keep up like that with the L-Bag. If you ever have trouble understanding what is going into the R-Bag, you can always ask and question why, what, when and how about anything! You are encouraged to do that, unlike questioning anything in the L-Bag.

Hmmmmmm…if you ever did that kind of questioning with L-Bag stuff, the admonishment is, "You dare not question these." These truths are ancient. *The real truth is: these much revered falsities are ancient.*

The disparity in the hypocritical treatment of the L-Bag and R-Bag is so smooth that everyone just sails through handling them that way all their life. Even the smartest of the smartest have trouble admitting that they were duped when they were so tenderly young. Say you put bad food in mouth, smell something gross, see something gruesome, or hear ear hurting sounds. You are allowed to spit bad food and walk away from other experiences. Not so with belief systems. You keep those inside and constantly spend time figuring how to justify them while the conflicts keep piling up.

Also, you start noticing some kids (which may include you) are positively excited about what is going in their R-Bags and how it is tickling all their extra brain spaces. You realize, if you are curious, there is no end to what can go into the R-Bag because the realities in the universe are just too many and their use and applications are even more numerous. Maybe these kids were all pre-mentored a bit before the time into preparation, consciously or otherwise, to expect exciting stuff for the R-Bag stuffing. If you were surrounded with all sorts of adults interested in Physics, Chemistry, Math, Biology and Zoology, astronomy, evolution, fossil hunting, and that kind of stuff, boy-o-boy were you lucky. They encouraged you to visit all sorts of museums on that kind of stuff—not just theme parks and famous ice cream shops and new "twist and shout" routines.

All this while, your L-Bag is getting stuffed very infrequently, maybe once a week on Sundays. Better know what is in it and it is slated to be your grave marker. Occasionally, someone dies, say after carrying his-her L-Bag for 70 to 90 years. If he is buried, the headstone will reflect probably only their L-Bag! If cremated, the notes somewhere will mention his belief system "given to him" at birth.

You bear the burden of carrying the L-Bag and R-Bag everywhere, but you do not mind because "your pride and flowering ego" is so fulfilled by the admirers surrounding you. People may envy you secretly when your R-Bag is filled with great stuff, but often the envy is based on what you have had in the L-Bag. How can someone raised in that faith can become such a great student of science? If you have nothing in your R-Bag, your L-Bag counts for zilch, anywhere you go. Stated another way, all the respect you get for the efforts you put to stuff the R-Bag adds respect and envy to your L-Bag. "Guess who's coming to dinner tonight"

The accolades galore when you are in a large crowd, all with the same type of L-Bags, but the admiration is directed because of how you are excelling in your R-Bag stuff, filled with Math, Science, Music, Sports, Instruments, Telescopes, Physics, Chemistry, Biology, Zoology, and so many others. Not a question about your L-Bag. Everything about it is assumed, even if you remember nothing from it anymore.

The adult at the pulpit who taught you the L-Bag stuff possibly is now never sure if what he taught you is relevant and real anymore. Long, long ago, all that supernatural stuff mixed with morals and ethics might have been OK when there was no one who confidently knew how to figure out this world, this universe, and all that is in it. **But today?** One can keep the good morals and ethics and dump the supernatural stuff while its artforms, culture, and music can continue to live as history and inspiration for new forms.

The absolute weakness of the L-Bag stuff shows when *someone has to argue* that it cannot be separated from good morals and ethics. Baaaaah Humbug, and you can say that again. The teacher trained to teach from the R-Bag has to keep upgrading his own R-Bag and renew it constantly and he must be silently doubting about his L-Bag stuff each time new stuff arrives into the R-Bag. L-bag stuff is to be doubted forever, R-bag stuff is true for ever, albeit adjusted occasionally. This sort of R-Bag stuff has become an absolute necessity to learn since about 500 years ago. Till then there was literally only one bag for everything for every commoner. If your R-bag is empty you are labeled "uneducated". Today, no way of getting around filling the R-Bag! To boot up matters, in many modern political systems, it is the law! *You have to go to school from* **6 to 18 at least.**

Everyone finds this R-Bag learning a difficult chore unless they were well prepared right from the get-go after birth by their adults. Learning about nature is lot more difficult than uttering some faith-based lines. Here onwards you are required to explore more of your brain's extra space in region 3. It is a lot different than manually plowing the field with dad as in old times, tending to your animals, crops, straightening the barn, etc. Such things were done for millennia, when nothing better was known, and *the muscular big bully did not let you do anything else.* By the way, the universe does not give a hoot whether you attend to your R-Bag or L-bag.

What makes this R-Bag learning difficult is that *it is truth-based knowledge about everything,* and one cannot simply think the way things are and say that is the truth. *All religious greats from eons ago are guilty of making this thinking process to be superior to observing, tinkering, evaluating and establishing the way the things really are.* A brick is a humble piece of earth shaped as you know it. Make billions of them and you can create any edifice of any size you desire based on your beliefs. *The greatest edifices do not make faith and belief right, and this edifice building has gone on far too long.*

The contents in the R-bag are the same all over the world for anyone, everyone, in what may be termed as the teachings from accredited schools, colleges, and universities. The same people who stuffed your L-Bag will insist that you fill your R-Bag too, never admitting that they were wrong with a lot of the stuff they put in your L-Bag. This R-Bag learning is called formal schooling. *Have any such good words for L-Bag stuff?*

Friendly arguments among clever scientists about what was in their R-Bags resulted in the spectacular "Solvay Conferences," and such get-togethers are so routine now. *Know anything about the first Solway conference or saw a photograph of it?*

You will love it if someone instilled in you the love of looking through a telescope in your backyard or a microscope in your study, just as someone like Mozart might love running a bow across a violin with exquisite control and precision. Just ask Neil deGrasse Tyson about who all inspired him as a young boy and how he finally took a trip to Carl Sagan's house for more inspiration. More likely than not, the same adults who partially corrupted you with L-Bag stuff will insist that you be good at what goes into the R-Bag for decades to come, so that you will get a good job, become famous, obtain better social status, and give them the opportunity to brag about how well you are earning and they may even take credit for how well you learned under their guidance *to fill up your R-Bag.*

They will never brag about what is in your L-Bag. *You never got a worthwhile diploma for that bag.* For all the 50 to 60 years or so that you work with your formal skills, your R-Bag stuff may be referred to and used in the running of some business, *as the play-book.*

Section 17: Science and Religion – Beyond the Polar Opposites

(Though it appears to this writer that Galileo fully doubted god-etc., he still outwardly accepted it. What else is one to do when threatened with death? The holy-person big-bully had in addition by now become the intimate friend of the muscular big-bully.) reposition

Some belief systems are so cocky that according to them there can *never be* another new belief system. The ego and stubbornness of homo-sapiens, no matter how saintly they are, have no bounds! Do they know that the earth has revolved around the sun for a mere 4 billion years and it still has 4 more billion years to go around? Does the "never"

Important science lesson: those who invented the processing and using of steam, its behavior, and its usefulness got the opportunity to create a plethora of words related to steam engines, trains, tracks, and other related inventions. Their language *focusing on science* of steam became the hub, spreading out new words into new worlds. *All dying languages must note this*. Latin is more fortunate because *its existing terminology* still gets used for new scientific words though the language itself in not used anymore. It goes to show how strong the influence a language has even after its death, when it focused on science, engineering and math for 100s of years. All homo-sapien groups pining for their ancient language to survive must note that they must embrace science fully to their core without hesitation. *If they want their language to survive and stay current that is the only way.* That way they will have the opportunity to create new words that the other languages can also borrow to use. They then get the opportunity to introduce new words. Words like "Chandrasekhar limit" (astronomy) or Tesla, Ampere, Volta (physics) are such examples. None of the previous words are Latin or any other language based but personality based but strictly from science and math side. Only due to religion and faith can groupism based on **god-etc.,** race, and ethnicity exist. With science, any sort of groupism sounds silly, unless an individual harbors religious, racial, or ethnic prejudice already. Only science gives a language to create new words and new art.

Any truth through science turns out to be the same for everybody and belongs exclusively to nobody. Security through religion, race, and ethnicity is temporary and unsatisfying. Security through science is permanent and it is true security. Yet no political system has been successful in convincing homo-sapiens at large to give up falsities from faith because such ignorance in homo-sapiens *is the bully-power for the elite in them*. Science cannot harbor prejudices, only inequality in knowledge, temporary for a lagging brain. For some budding scientists in certain regions, it is easier to "climb on other scientist's" shoulders" than it is for others in faraway regions. The more such things are equalized with no bigotry, the better it is for all the living.

Any prejudices in a true scientific way of thinking will become very quickly apparent. The brilliant Newton credited a few phenomena that he did not attempt to god's will, and that costed his non-revelations to be catapulted into the new realms of quantum mechanics. It is an enigma that he believed in god but his "Principia" is so much in total tune with scientific experiments, observation, new math and constant tinkering and questioning. He stood on great shoulders but none of them were brave enough to tell him to question the very validity of **god-etc**. That is how deep supernaturalness can be embedded even inside the most brilliant homo-sapiens.

Some of the finest qualities the homo-sapien has invented, and to a large extent cultivated while evolving using the large brain are: non-violence, empathy, and communal health care, anesthesia to relieve suffering for the many.

When "any preferred sayings" are passed on as holy and sacred, and accepted by the very young at a tender age below six, in the next generation they become inflexible laws for their descendants. Homo-sapiens *who were forced to convert* may have resisted, fought, and even gave their lives against conversion. But after a few generations, all is forgotten, so much as fully forgiven *and then fully embraced*. The converted fully accept the new ways of faith because someone had better swords, and that probably is the reason religious beliefs full of falsities are forced upon *the very young*, because they do not even have their tongues for meek weaponry. The history of black slaves and natives of Americas is a glowing testament to forced conversion into non-native supernatural beliefs and their full acceptance of those today. All of them are totally ignorant of the no-sense systems faith possess, and very often egotistically are belligerent defending.

The terrorists that fly planes into great structures hallucinate that they are going to paradise; little do they know or understand that **they were duped into believing that, though there is no such a place**, - even before they stopped sucking their thumbs.

Nothing gives more confidence to a homo-sapien in decision making than studying evidence based scientific phenomena and properly interpreting it for good actions beneficial to the homo-sapien living. Religion never gives you that confidence though the ignorant many will die backing it up for unverifiable benefits. One of the most dangerous situations that can be easily developed is convincing the poorest and least educated *billions* of the world to accept religion. Once faith sets into their minds and they accept it as their way of living, it is extremely difficult to convince them that what they have been taught is all wrong. Scores of languages have perished, and many cultures have perished, and this will continue so it will be to the hurtful feelings of many, *all because the languages and cultures described supernatural phenomena that never materialize into permanence.* The present languages heavy on such made up cultures based on faith will also disappear.

(The Fab-Four: Try to see it my way, do we have to keep on saying till you can't go on. Why do you see it your way? You're getting it wrong and selling your soul to the devilish side. You can't work it out, for life is so very short, and there is no time for that)

The new attitude of thinking, as it is now, is called the scientific way, or science. Trust the writer; **there will never be a new preacher of the ancient order again**, no matter how strongly foolish people proselytize. No preacher is ever coming back if he has promised to do so. *How can a monotheistic god be great when "that one" never existed and no one among trillions has ever seen him in real and* **describe him in unconditional uniformity** *of shape, form and looks?*

The homo-sapiens of today live divided and conflicted between the opposing poles of religion and science. The pole for religion is cold and unintelligible and full of falsities as per by those at the science pole. The science pole is warm and exciting—a habitat for curious researchers, excited explorers, and **constant collaborators** and the people at the religion pole pretend to shun them, but it won't be long before they switch their pole and turn it empty. Ask this writer, and he will unhesitatingly say: the homo-sapiens at the pole for religion should abandon it for good and move over to mingle with the "reasoning homo-sapiens" of the science pole, and they will be un-embarrassingly accepted.

Imagine there's no heaven, no hell below us, imagine there are no countries, and no religions too! And those most appropriate words slightly paraphrased came from John Lennon

What were the purposes and needs for better tools? Obviously, to kill game quickly and process it as a start. The killing of one's own kind for domination may not have arrived as an attitude yet on the scenes. The big-bullies, being the most skillful users of tools, ensured tight control over their groups and harems. That must have been the order of every day's hunt and trekking.

A modern-day incident of 140 years ago in the regions of East Africa might highlight the everyday routine of the down trodden homo-sapien groups *on the flat prairies*, on a daily basis 10 to 15 thousand years ago for hominins everywhere. A colonial country's colonizing force used indentured laborers from the African and Indian continents to build a lengthy railroad line north to south, not far from the border of the ocean near East Africa. The enslaved homo-sapiens slept in the open in tents at night. Two lions would routinely stealthily enter the tents and carry away one or two homo-sapiens, about 200 yards, and eat them in view to the horror of others in the tents witnessing, in the moonlit ambiance.

As mentioned, animals kill others only for 3 reasons: 1) Food, 2) Right to have sex, 3) Domain of territory. As a finality, the colonial master had to stand guard and shoot to kill both of the lions. These two lions, now stuffed to look real, are displayed in the museum of natural history in Chicago. Imagine the plights of bipeds and homo-sapiens for thousands of nights, day in and day out, if they had no choice but to sleep in the open.

Since religion started as a thought process that happened in the extra region of ones grown brain, it is definitely a 100% hallucination and remains so. Somehow it included morals and ethics, very early. Even as late as 5000 years ago in the religions of Africa along the Nile, not much morals and ethics must have been included in religion. What was included was the obsession with the big-bully's preservations of self into the imaginary afterlife and thus the reason for perpetual elaborate rituals. The writer wonders if both types of big-bullies ever thought "this is not moral and ethical to treat slaves so low". The ego of the pharaohs was so entrenched, they spent most of their life planning their womb to tomb pyramids.

This first "so-called" holy man could have been a homo-sapien, or a recent homo-penultimate (neanderthal?), or even one of the homo-*whatevers* prior to the homo-penultimate; can't say, but whatever he started with his imaginative ways to handle fears of homo-*whatevers* must have influenced all the tribes nearby so deeply that they made the preaching become a part and parcel of homo-sapien living. No homo-sapien ever thought of "checking out" the holy-man's hallucinations, maybe because it sounded so good and satisfying as presented by the charismatic 1st priest.

The very first fictional narration about the afterlife must have been a complete success for the narrator, with probably full acceptance. Since it was all innocent fiction coming from region 3 of brain, the story can be modified by others as they realized its essence, and *assuredly it did get modified again and again* and so today we have all the various religions. *Any pleasing thought-out* **solution to one's fears** *and misdeeds can be a part of religion.*

Hence, some supernatural beliefs do go extinct *by the simple saying* by former adherents, "- We do not believe in that anymore." Maybe this was the first time the zigzag backtracking travels of a particular group developed the zealous radial travel pattern and envisioned the total superiority of homo-sapiens (or homo-whatevers) with the of mission of proselytizing or killing non-believers. The zeal could have accelerated after the concept of "god" got introduced which slowly turned into **god-etc.** Interestingly, the emotional power of religion is so strong that after one's death, if there is a memorial, he might be fully preserved. The memorial is by what they were required to be by their religion chosen by others since birth, and not by what they did throughout their lives which normally accounts for 90% of their life.

Even if, and only if, there is such a thing / person as god, how does one know that there is only one god? Has anybody dared question those who believe to have been created by god, or are they so scared about death that they could be easily persuaded by a charismatic person? The more correct truth is that homo-sapiens created the idea of god out of thin air, not the other way. Science gives proof for all sorts of happenings in the universe and without ever the need to mention god. The word god should today be relegated to ancient history or better yet simply eliminated.

After "experimenting" with many, as well as many types of gods in various geographical locations, *charismatic leaders have strongly voiced that **there is only one god**.* This is because the preachers just thought that idea to be simpler, not because there was any proof, and further it is easier for the religious big-bullies to have control when only one god exists according to them, which is more difficult with polytheism. Baah-humbug OK, - for now one god, but he had different descriptions in different geographical locations. This one god principle never unites the various groups that all followed one god principle. By now, i.e., say 2000 years ago, it should have been possible for these monotheists homo-sapiens to describe fully this just one god. None of them could. What is the big deal about only one god, when science vehemently proves that "the one" should be more correctly a zero? Zero-theism or no-theism should be the rally cry going forward.

Religion claims to be fair, but it never is. Religion claims to be the truth, but it never is.

Every religion says *there is only one god, which is **their one god***. We actually have several of "one-gods" because he came out differently with differing hallucinations, and a hominin can hallucinate anything it wants. Science can never have two different of the same thing.

Great charismatic leaders with the powers of their brains in region 3, self-convinced, state that they are, *each one of them separately*, even when hundreds of years apart, *the true representatives of god,* but none of them seem to be able to describe this god in material form. They were able to get away saying such things then because their subjects were meek and ignorant, and the leaders were persistent in their gospels. Hubris, *hubris*, **hubris**. The combination of a large brain with large excess of brain power, not really needed to function as a mammal, creates huge egos and a huge capacity to hallucinate. Hence, each charismatic hallucinator claims he is the only one that knows the true path and some even claim confidently no one new will ever come out in the future to show a different way. It is the height of hubris, *hubris,* **hubris** and the partial truth is that, - yes no one new is ever coming back to preach because such person never existed anywhere.

The real antidote for this kind of absolutism is *the medicine of study of science,* prescribed by the scientists.

An interesting fact about supernatural beliefs is that they DO get superseded! Science's proofs and laws rarely get superseded unless some chinks in the armor of the homo-sapien tinkerer become bothersome. *Aristotle has been corrected so many ways.*

That "there is only one god, and further, he is so, as "I describe him" is the highest form of egotism that even the stated describer-scriber may not know exists within self.

Did that soothsayer have any idea, irrefutably, that the ground we, including him-, stand on is already over 4 billion years old, with reputedly a few billion more to go?

There is always the chance that a certain homo-sapien that has walked away to far-off distances will grow in brain size and capacity at a different rate than members of his own group or other groups. Hence, *differences in homo-sapiens individually or groupwise will always exist.* But still, They are our own kind and not to be bullied but to be looked at with compassion. In certain aspects, science is superior to a courtroom drama, though both rely heavily on evidence. A courtroom drama is totally in the hands of homo-sapiens; but facts and evidence can be fabricated through lies and prejudices in favor of either the defendant or the plaintiff. In science, this is not possible; the evidence has to exist in nature, the same for prosecution or defense.

Just as today, most who believe in god, etc., consider long abandoned beliefs as paganism, in due course, the beliefs of today will be considered as paganism in view of science. As Richard Dawkins points out, in a courtroom dealing with proving a murder case, no one may have seen the murder act, and hence no witness is available; but the prosecution brings on such a large amount of "circumstantial evidence" that 12 jurors or the judge is able to decide on the verdict. For religion the circumstantial evidence is zero to prove any belief it professes.

In a similar manner, in science, to prove an important point or disprove a wrongly held belief, a plethora of evidence is studied by many (a lot more than 12 jurors!), and then and only then, the judgements are accepted. Judgement for scientific cases is better than a homo-sapien courtroom for true or false *because nature does not cheat*. Newton was proved to be wrong only after his micrometer methods in science showed errors in his laws of motion when applied at the micrometer-scale. He had no access to studying such minute scaled happenings of nature. But at macro scale his intellectual findings still work and are accepted with no discernable error. Using the scientific way, it is possible to study anything: super-mini-micro, micro, normal-macro, super-large, living, and non-living.

Is there a better way for the growing brain to behave than train self to be scientific? Anyone today in any profession should ask themselves: how much do I use what I learned from 0 to about 6 years, and how much do I use what I learned any time after that in those secular schools?

Our body, by mass, is ~65% oxygen, 18.5% carbon, 9.5% hydrogen, 3.2% nitrogen, 1.3% calcium, 0.6% phosphorus. These six elements make up over 98% of the body's weight. Others making up the remaining 2% are potassium, sulfur, sodium, chlorine, etc. With barely 15 elements, our bodies make the trillions of cells with DNA, RNA, water, proteins, fats, sugars, etc., and everything needed by the static homo-sapien machine: the brain. All the efforts in explaining, and all the descriptions about the functioning of the universe, *were largely erroneous till they were clarified by the scientists of the last few hundred years*. The good honest scientist will explain what is known through evidence, and he will never try to push what is not known or not understood, except for saying so. But the egomaniacal big-bullies of religion, or the riches-seeking or power craving political big-bullies, will not agree to the ignorance they harbor. Too bad. The believer is too timid to leave a group and become an island in itself when needed to do so.

Homo-sapien is the first creature that noticed the benefits of slavery, in apposition to plain killing the inferior, and so *after he invented slavery, he boldly put it in books when writing was invented.* Slavery is not wholesome just because it appears in a holy-book and that should not be taken as an excuse to promote it anew. The so called holy-book is un-holy because slavery is included in it. Those who fought to eliminate it are the true holy-men.

Being an observer and experimentalist is far more superior to being an intellectual thinker because intellectuals often keep on hallucinating and arguing about useless stuff, whereas the experimentalist goaded by observations shows evidences through experiments and simply says, "There it is as I find it, QED" Faraday, only with couple years of schooling made all the electrical machinery you know possible, strictly by tinkering and observing with magnets and electrical batteries.

"The **god-etc.** methods asks you **NOT** to think or tinker, science etc. methods **REQUIRES** you to think and tinker." Polar opposites!

Individuals who believe and promote quack religious beliefs as cures will themselves seek treatment from the most scientific medical establishments when their health conditions need it. It is a hobby for people of various regions to keep on touting their natural remedies because it satisfies their pride and ego. But none of them will follow those remedies when push comes to shove with their own health.

Do you know of any kid who asks too many questions, even if many sound silly? Encourage the kid! Once the innocent curiosity of the young is destroyed and baseless beliefs in the supernatural ways are firmed up in him, the individual may not recognize his own ways into these false beliefs for their entire lifetime.

As often is the case, the big-bully can muscle into the brains of a scientist, forcing him to do his bidding for more dangerous weapons. Poison gas was a consequence in the Great War that pit good scientists against bad scientists who went to the side of evil for sake of politics of racial superiority. The truths of science will perpetually exist whether they are discovered or not and whether we homo-sapiens will exist or not, *but any truths claimed by the religious will die eventually* when discovered to be hoaxes, *by science!* This process of training the infants into more or less self-realized explorers of real-world and real universe must be the objective, while surely maintaining the preferred culture, language and arts. This is something that has to be constantly tackled by groups of like-minded individuals of many traditions. It is too big a task for well-meaning single individuals.

With no scientific process imagined or proposed by anybody, it must have been precarious living for most homo-*whatevers* when the holy men came onto the worldly scene. They had to agree with them. Looking back, proselytizing grew to become a subtle form of barbarism. But what if newfound uses of the brain's capacity show that all these believers of faith were all always wrong about **god-etc.?** No one is burning in Dante's inferno because there never was such place! If ever there was such a thing as an original sin, violence is it.

Religion thrives under muscular monarchy and the hypocrisy of superiority, competition, and elimination of non-believers, whereas science beams with sports-like friendly competition and all scientists accept proven results. Science simply explores how nature works and bravely attests its works will go on for billions of years. "Science observes, improves the observing tools, interprets the observations, lest anyone question and doubt the interpretations, encourages questions, and forces one to think *through*.

ONLY SCIENCE and math are the same for EVERYONE, and ANYTHING ELSE is different for everyone.

In science, if an ignorant person kicks up useless verbal dust, a thousand people with knowledge will clear the air. There are about 8.8 million active scientists, and it is not easy to fool them. With religion, people have been fooled just as soon as they were born by their adults, who were similarly fooled when they were born.

Section 18: Are you a Homo-Sapien Avatar?

This popular Sanskrit word avatar was often invoked in the writer's household. It has two connotations. First the positive, it refers to the appearance or apparition of god *in human form;* Second the negative, the apparition of the devil. Of course, at home we enjoyed using the 2nd connotation more often, especially when we wanted to talk about a relative we did not like, and there were a few of them.

(The word really should have been spelled uhvathaar=uh-va-thaar, to get the right pronunciation, uh, pronounced as the first syllable in um-brella, with very slight aspirated h, -va much like win won and -thaar rhymes with bar, the "th" being soft like in thin, thick, and not hard like in this, that)

There seems to be no doubts that the universe is about 13.7 billion years old, the solar system is about 9 billion years of age, and the earth is about 4.5 billion years old. The large Indian sub-continent broke off from Antarctica and traveled N E to bump against Tibet, about 40m years ago. This large region normally comprised of today's India, Pakistan, portions of Persia and a large section of Afghanistan, all of Hindukush, Himalayas and small countries nestled in them, Bangladesh, and portions of

Myanmar, Shri Lanka and myriads of small islands nestled in eastern portion of Indian ocean and the bay of Bengal. This region on the earth described above, is albeit often much neglected by the other more muscularly superior regions of the west. This geographical region is where the extra space in homo-sapien's brains (region 3) of the *local* charismatic homo-sapiens, long ago but yet within The Evolutionary Modern Era, opted their homo-sapienism *into the softer direction of cooperation, non-violence, persuasion, and accommodation (Hinduism, Jainism, and Buddhism)*. One can easily checkout this fact by studying the religions and cultures that emanated in the Indian sub-continent since eons ago and all three of them still exist today in full force. This region's philosophies are in opposition when compared to the *muscular big-bulliness of the west*. The west along with northern China and Mongols developed the most ferocious barbarians since thousands of years. **No such barbarians ever emanated in the Indian subcontinent!** This difference in history is not subtle! Those who killed others indiscriminately in the name of faith should note!

Frequent local quarreling and bickering was always there in the Indian subcontinent too, but it never amounted to much. By and large, any ancient philosophies and religions that emanated in this region, all gravitated toward non-violence, and mutual co-operation and accommodation. Here is the only region where one famous king Ashoka, when his ego got better of him, resorted to a high degree of killing, and soon after realized the brazenness in what he destroyed. *He then openly apologized* to all affected by the violent conflict and followed up by becoming completely pacifistic for the rest of his life. Does such an example of repentance exist elsewhere with a major king *anywhere?* This writer thinks not. Such is the power of the hold of ego on a homo-sapien that makes an apology almost impossible.

A region focusing on non-violence as a core philosophy as is the Indian subcontinent is vulnerable to barbarism from its surrounding regions, and indeed, it did become vulnerable and was subjugated a few times. Being non-violent is considered to be such a weakness! (Ask Gandhi)

For the writer, who does not believe in god or the devil, the word "avatar" is important only for this write-up, only for its meaning as it is often still used in normal conversations.

If one did not like a particular homo-sapien, and he was approaching, it is very common to say, "We have the devil's avatar showing up." The great holy positive avatars (such as Raamaa and Krishnaa) are quoted less often in conversations, because they have god related religious connotations from higher up.

The ancient "wise and holy" homo-sapiens from the regions of the Indian subcontinent described the appearances of god, the creator descending to the earth from heavens, to be in the form of avatars, *the purpose being generally to straighten out misbehaving homo-sapiens.* Here below the writer shows how incredibly accurate these ancient Indians were in relation to describing the actual order of avatars, when comparing to evolutionary history of life as presented by science of today. The ancient *rishis* of the Himalayas (presumably) quoted the avatars that descended on to earth in this order:

- The 1st avatar is the fish (Matsya avatar), and this matches with science, that life started and proliferated in the seas billions of years ago,

- The 2nd avatar is a tortoise, an amphibian, (Kurma avatar), and Tiktaalik, as described by Shubin, about it 380 m years ago reasonably matches,

- The 3rd avatar is a boar, a mammal (Varaha avatar); here science quotes reptiles to come next, a small mismatch,

- The 4th avatar is a combo of man-lion (Narasimha avatar) Some fair matching with science of mammals leading to homo-sapiens. This even matches some very ancient cave graffiti and artifacts.

- The 5th is the early homo-sapien (Vaamana avatar) matches with science of homo-sapiens,

- The 6th is an advanced muscular homo-sapien with powerful tools (Parshurama avatar)

- **The 7*th* avatar is the writer's most ideal homo-sapien** since he by self never claimed to be a god (Raamaa avatar)

- The 8th is Krishnaa, who openly claimed to be god, and since the writer does not believe in **god-etc.**, he is not considered to be ideal by the writer; and so on, there are one or two more avatars not important for our write-up.

You will notice that the avatar order by ancient Indians did match the science of evolution to a surprising extent.

This writer believes that all avatars were invoked in The Evolutionary Modern Era, may be 5000 to 4000 years ago.

The character of Raamaa, who to the writer is the most ideal homo-sapien, will be referred to in the rest of this write-up with reverence, with explanations. Raamaa never claimed to have descended from god and that suits fine with the writer's philosophy, though he is considered a god-descendent by millions of homo-sapiens to this day.

THE KITH AND KIN OF HANUMAAN

You are of course allowed to have your own ideal hero homo-sapien of your choice.

Since one's life's experiences, if based upon falsities of belief in supernatural, and those do vary widely between cultures, religions, and political forms, - one's internal conflict never ceases until one does away with such beliefs as to be errors and embraces the reality of reasoned truths.

Both of Avatars of Raamaa (earlier) and Krishnaa (later) are even now-today worshipped as "gods" by, say about a billion people. Of course, this writer has no god relationship with them except admitting that they both were exceptional homo-sapiens. Raamaa never claimed to be god incarnate though such connotations are given to him and is heavily prevalent today. But, Krishnaa fell into the standard trap of a prophet of believing himself to be god incarnate, and that diminishes his status *for this writer* in relation to Raamaa. Unquestionably both were extremely worldly-wise and lived lives to the benefit and directives of homo-sapiens.

Raamaa was raised in royal courts as to be a legitimate king, and Krishna's long story is that he was raised as a commoner. **Their stories are epics in the region of the original Indian subcontinent** which would encompass India, Pakistan, Bangladesh, Large parts of Afghanistan, various small countries in the Himalayas, portions of Hindukush, Tibet, Shri Lanka and various nearby islands all along the coasts, and large parts of Myanmar. This was a very large land area indeed that worshipped both Raamaa and Krishnaa as god-incarnates for a long time till barbarians with weapons crossed over.

You cannot stop millions of homo-sapiens of today (the writer excluded) considering Raamaa to be god incarnate. Occasionally the believers in supernatural give every once-in-a-while someone new the title of *god is emerging as a new latter day charismatic saint,* but their preaching material in general is the same as produced in the two epics and the Vedaas.

Raamaa's closest friend and closest disciple after his brother Lakshmanaa was **Hanumaan, the monkey** (also given the status of god and an avatar by a billion or so devotees). Though he is not given status as an avatar by some others, he is worshipped as a god (again, the writer is excluded). He is the only animalistic deity given an individual worshipping *mandhir* (temple) of his own with no other deity present, - in general.

It is called Hanumaan Mandhir and extremely common place of worship as far as temples go.

In fact, that Hanumaan as a devotee of Raamaa is so revered by the believers of Raamaa. In every Raamaa Mandhir (temple) invariably with the standing trinity of Raamaa, Seethaa (his wife), and Lakshmanaa (his brother), Hanumaan is always depicted kneeling at the feet of

Raamaa. What better guesswork can you ask of the ancients of this region whose intellect explained the almost correct evolutionary stages of all creatures in avatar form, starting in the seas, *and culminating to us homo-sapiens so fairly accurately and chose the famous monkey Hanumaan to be Raamaa's best friend?* We did evolve out of primates, did we not? In such an environment of Raamaa and Hanumaan, never a "kill them all" type barbarian ever emanated from the philosophies and religions from the Indian subcontinent. *There is no other region on the earth that can lay such a claim.*

The writer's summary of our evolution into homo-sapiens is " **We all are the kith and kin of Hanumaan**".

Raamaa, the greatest homo-sapien of all time, the most revered king of the ancient and really large Indian sub-continent, never bullied anyone. In true great homo-sapien fashion he lived all the life required of royalty and also of the normalcy of a regular homo-sapien. In addition, he struggled with the standard deviousness of his relatives like most homo-sapiens do. For quirky reasons that he could not escape, they ordered him as penance to live in the forest incognito for years on end as punishment and payment. He accepted and complied.

His devout brother and devout wife decide to give him perpetual company in the forest, where he gets subjected to the horror of his wife being stolen by the supposedly most devious and powerful character of the Raamaayanaa

Epic. That devilish persona is that of Raavanaa, from Shri-Lanka. Here is where Hanumaan, the monkey hero, enters the scene in the epic, and he becomes instant devotee of Raamaa *earning Raamaa's undying trust.* Hanumaan is instrumental in leading Raamaa and Lakshmanaa and a few other helpers to invade Shri-Lanka to rescue Seetha, where she is being held as a hostage by Raavanaa. Raavanaa fondest desire was that Seethaa will give up the insecurity with Raamaa and shift to his side. No sireeeee sir, nothing like that can ever happen in the heart of a noble homo-sapiens like Seethaa!

This whole story of these characters may be a myth and it truly is an ancient Epic, but if one removes any god-etc. and the supernatural that has been artificially inserted, *the life story of Raamaa and Hanumaan becomes most exemplary for any homo-sapien.*

We are all the kith and kin of Hanuman (the saintly Indian chimp) — no doubts for the writer about that.

Did Raamaa know he is also kith and kin of Hanumaan? Probably not, but we know of us that today?

Section 19: Is There a Better Way to Rid Falsities

So many of us are educated *only to earn that paycheck,* and pay no attention at core levels to the well-established evolutionary theories and thereby do not help to eradicate from deep inside us the **god-etc.** beliefs. Such eventually *lead to conflicts and killings* for baseless reasons. Further danger is that all the big-bullies constantly curry the favor of the poor, uneducated, - the most vulnerable votes into their side.

The real and *ever-present culture* in all the homes ought to be towards mentoring the little one, who may not have the intelligence and experiences yet, into becoming curious explorers of the real and natural world. Any overt or silent non-belief in natural sciences and belief in *any type of* religious dogma that parents harbor will only be to the detriment of the child's intellectual growth and increase his future conflicts.

The child should be raised to explore and question anything and such attitudes by him should have no impediments. Too many no-no-no-no's and don'ts from caretakers, rather than "Would you like to try this?" "How about trying that?" and so on, will stunt the child's curiosity. The constant questioning will try the patience and biases of the caretakers but the discomforts of facing a questioning child must be born. The universe is the way it is, and get to know it standing on shoulders of others who have explored it in depth and now do your own studies. Look for evidence in multitude of directions and through other likeminded homo-sapiens and be convinced the greatness in life. The child will understand and relish these challenges. In just trying to disprove somebody builds the strength of finding truth.

If the homo-sapien-created art forms and music are your thing, then let that be so, but no more serious supernatural hallucinations in the new art form except in the form for fiction and entertainment.

The child must never feel that he is learning anything unnatural because there isn't any unnaturalness in evidence found in nature. Except for morals and ethics, the child's *the L-Bag should stay empty*. Since the child is already learning truths of homo-sapiens and the universe, there is zero chance that he will ever be conflicted in using brain's region 3 in understanding anything and everything.

Do teach the child in the manners of, - the greatness of the great homo-sapiens *of the past* eons, and that they should be respected **but only in a historical context**. Many great homo-sapiens of late have already paid the high price in trying to correct the ancients that were on the wrong side. Copernicus, Galileo, and Darwin, all of them with many others had death threats. Einstein, even if he gave the euphemistic answers such as "god does not play dice…" or "I believe in Spinoza's god", etc., - in the writer's mind, by the time of his death he must have known 100% that there is no such a thing as god. It must have been political for him not to say so, so bluntly.

Often, it is the parents" wise intervention against the norm of the group with beliefs in faith, that created the greatest freedom of thought for the child and led the child to become a greatest scientist. Faraday's mother removed him from school from an unreasonable teacher, and that was a courageous act, giving Faraday the freedom to become one of the foremost experimenters of electricity and magnetism. Our own Richard and David Attenborough's upbringing by their highly educated parents *appears to have leaned well* into their present day evolutionary natural living. Is there a more qualified homo-sapien than Sir David to tout constantly to keep our natural world better than it is, and some one better than Sir Richard to introduce us to the long extinct dinosaurs?

How can one do justice for one's secular education?

- ***know that there never were such things as god, and god-etc.*** and support the…

- Erasure of religious statements such as "In God We Trust", especially off of currency notes;

- Stop saying "so help me god" or "may god help you" or "may god help this country",

- Stop saying "for heaven's sake" or "we will pray for you" or "may god bless you",

- *And any similar false statement attributable to the supernatural.*

This very difficult system of eliminating **god-etc.**, from the homo-sapien's mind and reformulating it into a mind based on reasoning all about reality seems only to be accomplished slowly by enough well-meaning, wise, agreeable, and knowledgeable *global* homo-sapiens. We need the full support of many new parents-to-be, agreeing to raise kids right from the start of their living, on a life based on nature-created world. ***No god whatsoever,*** but for historical perspective only.

Achieving a world full of homo-sapiens that live by reason and nature is indeed a monumental task: This has to be a worldwide task with solid well thought of teachings which do not encroach on anyone's culture or identity.

Ever since the creation of the most destructive weapons some 80 to 85 years ago, homo-sapiens are in a lull, thinking no one will ever use them. Homo-sapiens who know how to make such weapons will only increase in number one way or some other way, and it may take only one person's insulted ego or deranged mind for ballistic bombs of the most destructive kind to be deployed. The uneasiness of religious aggression seems to exist perpetually because supernatural beliefs seem to have existed for ever. Only when homo-sapiens are rid of such beliefs, then and only then, will the uneasy aggression based on religion will disappear.

END of Write-Up

xxxxxxxxxxxxxxxxxxxxxxxxxxxxxxxxxxxxxxxxxxxxxx